Hellman
in Hollywood

Hellman
in Hollywood

Bernard F. Dick

Rutherford ● Madison ● Teaneck
Fairleigh Dickinson University Press
London and Toronto: Associated University Presses

© 1982 by Associated University Presses, Inc.

Associated University Presses, Inc.
4 Cornwall Drive
East Brunswick, NJ 08816

Associated University Presses Ltd
27 Chancery Lane
London WC2A 1NF, England

Associated University Presses
Toronto M5E 1A7, Canada

Library of Congress Cataloging in Publication Data

Dick, Bernard F.
   Hellman in Hollywood.

   Bibliography: p.
   Filmography: p.
   Includes index.
   1. Hellman, Lillian, 1906–   —Moving-picture plays.
2. Hellman, Lillian, 1906–   —Film adaptations.
3. Film adaptations.   4. Moving-picture authorship.
I. Title.
PS3515.E343Z63   1982   812′.52   81-72044
ISBN 0-8386-3140-1   AACR2

Printed in the United States of America

Contents

Preface

In the introduction to *Scoundrel Time*, Garry Wills called Lillian
Hellman "not only the leading woman playwright of our time, but of
our nation's entire history." Although one tends to be suspicious of
definitive judgments, Wills's claim is probably the least contest-
able statement in his introduction. Zoë Akins and Rose Franken
were not in Hellman's league, nor, for that matter, were Rachel
Crothers and Zona Gale; had she not died so young, Lorraine
Hansberry might have been. Perhaps Wendy Wasserstein and Beth
Henley, whose *Crimes of the Heart* won the 1981 Pulitzer Prize for
drama, might surpass her. If so, the claim would have to be
modified; but for the present it stands. No American female playwright has achieved Hellman's international reputation, and few
writers of either sex have been popular enough to merit a five-part
interview on public television, as Hellman did in 1980.

A writer acquires a reputation like Hellman's through an ability
to impinge upon the literary, political, and cultural life of the
times, producing works that find a place in the annals of literature
and the pages of history. In the case of a dramatist, this means
writing plays that receive major revivals on Broadway, off Broadway, and in regional theater. Hellman has seen important revivals
of all but one of her plays in her own lifetime.[1] But it also means
becoming one of history's vectors, intersecting with time and leaving behind a permanent mark of that encounter. Hellman's name
will always be associated with the McCarthy era, if not for *Scoundrel Time*, then for the sentence in her famous 1952 letter to the
House Committee on Un-American Activities that has become one
of the most memorable quotations of the century and, as Dr. Johnson would have said, part of the literary *parole:* "I cannot and will
not cut my conscience to fit this year's fashions."

It was a simple but powerfully turned phrase with a metaphor
familiar enough to evoke the spontaneous image of a universal

9

conscience cut from the pattern of humanity. Since Hellman labored over the letter, one assumes the aphorism did not come about in an intuitive flash. To Hellman, at least the Hellman of the plays, writing is a craft, a skill; what Aristotle called a *techne* and Horace, an *ars*. It is the technique of linking events in a causal and temporal nexus; it is the art of creating drama from that nexus; it is the skill of guiding an action to a climax; it is the ability to prune away excess through constant rewriting.

Hellman's screenplays evidence the same art. Ordinarily one does not associate Hellman with the movies, yet before she became a dramatist, she was a reader—or, as the position is sometimes designated today, a story analyst—at Metro-Goldwyn-Mayer (MGM). After the success of her first play, *The Children's Hour*, she became a screenwriter for Samuel Goldwyn, proving that the skills learned in the theater could be transferred to film.

Essentially, Hellman approached screenwriting as she did play writing; she favored linear structure and the interlocking of action and character. Hellman is a realist in the sense that she respects objective reality although she will reshape and rework it. Since description was never her forte, she reduced character to language, which she refined until the dialogue was able to transmit the drama by itself. Whatever limitations the theater imposed on her she accepted as conventions, working within them to create what the classical critics have called the semblance of truth, the representation of reality. When she became a screenwriter, she accepted the even greater limitations of film, leaving room within the narrative for the visuals to complete what language could not.

Hellman has written little about her art, preferring to practice it rather than theorize about it. However, in a revealing passage in *Pentimento*, she described how she brought Anouilh's *L'Alouette* to Broadway as *The Lark*, turning "bubble glory stuff," as she called it, into the first success Jean Anouilh ever had in America. She did not alter Anouilh's basic metaphor of history refracted through the prism of theater. She merely made it a dramatic metaphor by adding dialogue that was realistic, even slangy, and turning the second act debate on authority versus submission into a clash of wills between the Inquisitor, who represents the church, and Joan, who represents man. Twenty years earlier, in 1935, Hellman did the same in her first screenplay, *The Dark Angel*, which was also an adaptation; she relieved the original of the heavy symbolism that hung over it like a dome, thereby freeing the drama within.

Lillian Hellman is a natural subject for a film study. In addition to having been an adapter and, on one occasion, an original screenwriter, she has also seen her work brought to the screen by others. She adapted three of her own plays *(The Children's Hour* as *These Three, The Little Foxes,* and *The Searching Wind)* and three works by other authors *(The Dark Angel* from Frances Marion's 1925 scenario, Sidney Kingsley's *Dead End,* and Horton Foote's *The Chase).* Other screenwriters were responsible for *Watch on the Rhine, Another Part of the Forest,* the second version of *The Children's Hour, Toys in the Attic,* and *Julia.* Sometimes the screenwriters failed *(The Children's Hour, Toys in the Attic);* once, the adaptation was an improvement on the original *(Julia).*

Every film adaptation involves a set of basic questions, the most important of which is whether the adaptation has achieved as cinema what the original had achieved as literature. Or, if the original was minor literature, did film raise it to a level it could not otherwise have reached? Conversely, if the film version fell short of the original, was it because the original realized its excellence in its own medium? A study of the Hellman screenplays, both her own and those based on her work, offers some answers to these complex questions.

Teaneck, New Jersey

Acknowledgments

I wish to express my gratitude to Arlene and Alan Alda for obtaining the script of *Julia* for me; Lelia Alexander for describing how she researched *The North Star;* Ted Chesler, Chairman of the Communications Department at Fairleigh Dickinson University (Teaneck-Hackensack Campus), for his generosity in renting Hellman's Goldwyn films for me; my honors student Brian Dauth for some valuable discussions of *These Three* and *The Children's Hour;* Claire Dudley, Media Librarian at Fairleigh Dickinson, for arranging screening facilities for me; Horton Foote for explaining how *The Chase* became a film; Michael Gordon for his detailed letter on the filming of *Another Part of the Forest;* Lillian Hellman for graciously answering my letters although she was recuperating from eye surgery; Sam Marx for describing to me over the telephone what it was like to be a reader at MGM in the early 1930s; my former student Martin Nocente for helping me see *The Chase* from a different perspective; Terry T. Roach and her exemplary staff at the Margaret Herrick Library of the Academy of Motion Picture Arts and Sciences, where research is a sinful pleasure; Emily Sieger of the Motion Picture Section of the Library of Congress for providing ideal facilities for viewing the films; Sister Jeanne Tierney, C.S.J.P. of St. Peter's College at Englewood Cliffs for tracking down the books I needed.

Some acknowledgments cannot be made in alphabetical order. I owe a special debt to my wife, Katherine Restaino, for spending her vacation poring over clippings and threading moviolas.

Hellman
in Hollywood

1

From Sam Marx to Sam Goldwyn

At the start of the 1930s, Arthur Kober and his wife were living in a ramshackle house on Long Island. While Mrs. Kober was trying unsuccessfully to write short stories, Arthur was working as a Broadway press agent. His current assignment was promoting Marc Connelly's new play, *The Green Pastures*, which was scheduled to open on 26 February 1930. However, Arthur really considered himself a writer, and soon he would be one. Before the end of the decade, Arthur Kober would write one of the best-remembered comedies of the 1930s, *Having Wonderful Time* (1937); he would also be known as the creator of Bella Gross, the Bronx girl searching for "Mr. Right," whom he immortalized in his *New Yorker* sketches.

In 1930, Mrs. Kober was also on the threshold of fame; in four years she would write a play that would establish her as a major American dramatist. But as the 1930s began, the Kobers' literary credentials were unimpressive. Arthur had been a columnist for the *New York Morning Telegraph* and the *New York Evening Sun;* his wife had published nine book reviews in the *New York Herald Tribune* and a story in *Paris Comet*. Then, shortly before *The Green Pastures* premiere, Arthur's fortunes changed when Paramount Pictures offered him a screenwriting job at $450 a week.

In 1930, $450 was an impressive salary for a neophyte. Two years later, MGM would hire William Faulkner at $500 a week, despite the fact that he had already written *Sartoris* (1929), *The Sound and the Fury* (1929), *As I Lay Dying* (1930), and *Sanctuary* (1931).[1] And in 1933, Columbia Pictures would offer Nathanael West $350 a week, even though he had just published *Miss Lonelyhearts* (1933) which Twentieth Century—Fox purchased immediately upon publication and filmed under the title *Advice to the Lovelorn* (1933).

Arthur accepted the job at Paramount even though it meant moving to the west coast. However, Mrs. Kober was reluctant to leave New York. When Arthur departed for Hollywood after completing publicity for *The Green Pastures*, she remained on Long Island. Eventually, she would join her husband in Hollywood, but not for several months. Such separations were not uncommon with the Kobers, who were accustomed to living apart for long periods. When Arthur took a job with *Paris Comet*, Mrs. Kober traveled around Europe. In 1929, she worked for four months as a publicist for a stock company in Rochester, New York; she spent the summer of that year in Bonn, Germany—alone. Although she would later call her seven years (1925–32) with Arthur "pleasant" and would praise her husband as "kind" and "generous," she clearly regarded their marriage as a casual relationship rather than a union of man and wife.

There was another reason that she did not leave for California with her husband. Procrastination was part of a behavior pattern that started five years earlier and manifested itself in periods of aimlessness and indecision. She drifted from one job to another, from editorial assistant to play reader to publicist. As a child, she wanted to be a writer and even recorded her observations in a writer's book so they would be available when she needed them. At twenty-four, she still wanted to be a writer, but of what she was uncertain. Short stories were not her strong point; the more she tried to write them, the more frustrated she became. By the fall of 1930, she was restless and eager for a change. After closing up their Long Island home, Lillian Hellman Kober followed her husband to the West Coast—a trip that took five days and two trains to make.

Since Arthur was financially cautious, the Kobers' first home in Hollywood was a one-room apartment on Sunset Boulevard. Then, when he felt more secure in his job, they moved to the Garden of Allah, a Hollywood hotel popular with screenwriters and resembling a Moroccan villa with stucco bungalows and palm trees. Finally, they rented a house above Hollywood Boulevard that was so ugly it only intensified Lillian Hellman's malaise. Feeling uprooted as well as aimless, she read during the day and drank at night. Arthur, who had found his wife jobs in the past, realized he would have to do so again.

MGM's story editor at the time was Sam Marx, who had known the Kobers in New York. When Arthur prevailed upon Marx to find his wife a job, arguing that his marriage was at stake, Marx tested her for a position in the reading department. Each of the major studios had a story editor who looked for suitable properties, as well as a staff of readers who synopsized them, sometimes also commenting on their screen potential. In its heyday, the reading department at MGM handled 20,000 pieces of literature a year, ranging from magazine articles to novels in galley. The readers were tested for their ability to write clear and accurate summaries of the material. Marx was so impressed by Hellman's test that he hired her immediately, at the magnificent salary of $50 a week.

Hellman described her stint at MGM in her first memoir, *An Unfinished Woman* (1969). Since she openly admits a poor memory for details, her account is understandably sketchy. Marx would take issue with her picture of the MGM reader as a synopsis writer of "idiot-simple" plot summaries for Louis B. Mayer. And while the writers' building was a two-story barracks that Dore Schary remembers as a "firetrap" and Hellman as a "rickety building on stilts," Marx maintains that the readers at least had access to a room with a library and deep leather chairs.[2]

Hellman's view of Hollywood was undoubtedly colored by her unhappiness there—an unhappiness that was both personal and professional. Despite her Southern origins, she was a typical New York intellectual with a bias against the movies. Yet when she began writing screenplays in the mid 1930s, she showed, in her very first script, that she had mastered an art that had eluded Fitzgerald and Faulkner. Unlike many of the other exiles in the sun, Hellman did more than merely "work on" scripts; she wrote them. Although Hollywood would never be her home, she discovered, like Ben Hecht, that the key to maintaining one's integrity as a writer while working in the movies was to spend as little time as possible in southern California.

Lillian Hellman has always been known for her sense of responsibility. Thus, during her stay at MGM, she did not shortchange the studio. Each morning she dutifully reported for work, checked the material that was piled on the table in the reading room, and turned out what Sam Marx called "beautiful" synopses. It was not a long drive from Hollywood to the MGM lot in Culver City, but it terminated in unreality—at a white colonnade that stretched for almost half a mile along Washington Boulevard. Such was MGM's imperial facade: fake marble columns of plaster and wood concealing acres of sound stages resembling four-story cardboard boxes, and buildings with long balconies and iron railings that gave the impression of a "perpetual tightrope," as Fitzgerald observed in *The Last Tycoon* (1941). To one film historian, MGM "from the outside looking in . . . has the air of the world's most exclusive country club, but from the inside it can have the air of a prison camp."[3]

The air also reeked of caste. The producers had fourteen-carat gold name plaques on their doors while the writers' names were typed on cards. A similar distinction prevailed in the MGM commissary, where writers such as Dorothy Parker, Ogden Nash, Frances and Albert Hackett, and George Oppenheimer occupied a table against the wall while the producers lunched in the center of the room. It was quite the reverse of the Round Table at the Hotel Algonquin where Robert Benchley, Marc Connelly, Dorothy Parker, George S. Kaufman, and other wits occupied a table in the middle of the room, surrounded by smaller ones where the less privileged sat in awe.

In 1930, Hellman was not even a writer, just a lowly reader. So, rather than walk into the commissary where the men who knew her husband would rise reluctantly when she passed by, Hellman preferred to lunch on the backlot, surrounded by sets of ancient Rome and modern London.

Even more frustrating than a segregated commissary was the lack of intellectual companionship. Craving intelligent conversation, she tried to strike up a friendship with another reader at MGM, Wilson Follett, best known for *Modern American Usage* (1966) which he began in 1958 and which Jacques Barzun and others completed after his death in 1963. It seemed incomprehensible to Hellman that a Harvard cum laude who had taught at Dartmouth College and Brown University and worked as an editor at Yale University Press and Knopf would be reading movie material. However, Follett had good reason for maintaining a low profile and discouraging Hellman's gesture of friendship. Having left his wife for his former secretary, he sought anonymity. "The reading department provides me with a marvelous refuge," he explained to Sam Marx.[4]

Hellman could no more understand that kind of thinking than she could the willingness of the readers to work for $50 a week. When she tried to organize them, Dorothy Pratt, who headed the reading department at MGM, delivered an ultimatum to Sam Marx: Pratt or Hellman. There was no need for Ms. Pratt to leave. After about a year, Hellman could no longer bear to make the trip to Culver City. Yet, in its own way, Hollywood was shaping her destiny. Had she not followed her husband to the west coast, she probably would never have met the man she later called "my closest, my most beloved friend"—Dashiell Hammett, who had already written such classics of detective fiction as *The Dain Curse* (1929) and *The Maltese Falcon* (1930). It was Hammett who, as we shall see, suggested the plot for her first play.

Hellman left Hollywood in 1932. When she returned three years later, it was not to MGM in dusty Culver City, but to Samuel Goldwyn's studio on Formosa Avenue; and it was not as a reader at $50 a week but as a screenwriter at $2500. She was no longer Mrs. Arthur Kober, but Lillian Hellman, author of the Broadway hit *The Children's Hour*, which was still running when she arrived in Los Angeles. Mrs. Arthur Kober might have to live in Hollywood, but Lillian Hellman could afford a house on the Pacific Palisades with a soda fountain in the basement. It seems as if her life were conforming to the conventions of an obscurity-to-fame scenario.

For eight years—"good years" as she called them in *Pentimento* (1973), her second memoir—Hellman enjoyed her association with Goldwyn until *The North Star* (1943) brought it to a painful end. However, at the beginning, she was fond of the producer and his studio, which was much friendlier than MGM. At least the Goldwyn commissary had a table reserved for the screenwriters. Hellman enjoyed lunching there, and with good reason: the food was excellent because Goldwyn believed his employees deserved the best, even if it meant hiring a top level chef to provide it.

Hellman arriving in Hollywood in 1935 to work as screenwriter for Samuel Goldwyn. *(United Press International)*

It was logical that Hellman would work for Goldwyn; he respected writers, or at least professed to. Whether he held them in as high esteem as his publicity releases claimed he did is problematical. At any rate, Goldwyn Pictures Corporation was no sooner formed in 1916 than full-page announcements appeared in the trade papers claiming that the company had "the ablest and most popular writers in the world." It certainly did not have the ablest and most popular stars, a factor that might explain Goldwyn's decision to concentrate on scripts.

In 1919, Goldwyn announced the formation of Eminent Authors,

Samuel Goldwyn (1882–1974), the producer for whom Hellman wrote five screenplays. *(Samuel Goldwyn Productions)*

Inc., a producing unit within the Goldwyn Corporation where authors would adapt their own works for the screen and receive top billing for their efforts. By literary standards, the original eminent authors were hardly eminent: Rex Beach, Gertrude Atherton, Mary Roberts Rinehart, Rupert Hughes, Gouverneur Morris, Basil King, and Leroy Scott. If Goldwyn believed Eminent Authors, Inc. would bridge the gap between literature and film, he did not understand the auctorial ego. The writers charged the scenario department with reducing their scripts to a few intertitles; the scenario department replied that the scripts were too wordy for silent films. Occasionally, Goldwyn would mediate and lecture his writers on the need to produce filmable scripts.

Had Eminent Authors, Inc. succeeded, it would have meant the end of the star system, or rather, the beginning of a different pantheon with the screenwriter as star. Still, Goldwyn never abandoned hope of attracting distinguished writers to Hollywood. With the advent of sound, a script was no longer a scenario with plot points and intertitles; it was a true screenplay with the action conveyed through dialogue. Therefore, whenever he could, Goldwyn signed up authors who knew how to construct a plot with a beginning, middle, and end and who could write intelligent dialogue. These authors were frequently playwrights: Elmer Rice (*Street Scene*, 1931; *Counsellor at Law*, 1933), Sidney Howard (*Dodsworth*, 1936), Ben Hecht and Charles MacArthur (*Barbary Coast*, 1935; *Wuthering Heights*, 1939), and Robert E. Sherwood (*The Best Years of Our Lives*, 1946).

In 1935, Goldwyn, complaining that writers regarded Hollywood as a stopover between projects, argued that the movie industry must "show writers that they can make as much out of a fine picture as they would from a successful play."[5] That same year, as if to prove his point, he hired Lillian Hellman.

Although Hellman was hired on the strength of *The Children's Hour*, her first assignment was not to adapt her play for the movies—that would come the following year—but to do the screenplay of *The Dark Angel* (1935), which Goldwyn had made a decade earlier as a silent. Since Goldwyn considered Hellman a novice at screenwriting, he assigned her a collaborator, the British playwright Mordaunt Shairp. Even though the credits for *The Dark*

Angel list Hellman and Shairp as coauthors, Hellman claims that Shairp's contribution consisted mostly of suggestions but that the screenplay was 90 percent hers.[6]

It is also a screenplay that Hellman has virtually ignored. In *Pentimento*, she does not even mention the title, calling it only "an old silly." But it was an old silly that had two previous incarnations: a 1925 Broadway play and a 1925 silent movie, both entitled *The Dark Angel*. The play, written by H. B. Trevelyan (pseudonym of Guy Bolton), was one of those wet, stoic British dramas, too arch for the boudoir, too humorless for the drawing room, but ideal for the parlor where, appropriately enough, the last act is set. It was the kind of play that smelled of tea roses and port, where the characters had the names of manors rather than people, and where the dialogue was so tinder-dry that the worst pun or the dullest metaphor would kindle it, creating more smoke than flame.

After the smoke had cleared, all that remained were the charred bones of the plot: a World War I romance between a British army captain and a peer's daughter. When a canceled leave prevents Captain Hilary Trent and Kitty Fahnestock from marrying, they repair to the local inn where they consummate their union and vow eternal fidelity. Kitty, however, has a presentiment of doom. Mixing her metaphors a bit, she recounts a dream in which "a cloud of birds" hovering over a battlefield suddenly metamorphosed into a host of angels who became tutelary spirits for some of the soldiers, but not for Trent. His is a dark angel. When Trent did not return from the war, Kitty assumed he had encountered the angel of death. After five years of mourning, she is about to marry Gerald Shannon when she learns that Trent is alive. What she does not know is that he is also blind. Rather than return to civilian life as a disabled veteran, he retired to a cottage and wrote boys' books under a pseudonym. Torn between her love for Shannon and her old vow of fidelity, Kitty calls on Trent, who magnanimously releases her from her pledge, leaving her free to marry Shannon.

In 1925, Goldwyn purchased *The Dark Angel* as a vehicle for his latest discovery, the Hungarian actress Vilma Banky. Believing the play would make a successful "weepie," he entrusted the adaptation to veteran screenwriter Frances Marion, who managed to make the plot less British without altering the setting. She started with the names. The Fahnestocks became the Vanes, and Kitty's father a Hubert rather than an Evelyn. Hilary was renamed Alan. Americans would clearly be more comfortable with an Alan Trent and a Kitty Vane than a Hilary Trent and a Kitty Fahnestock. The names were also more suited to the leads, Ronald Colman and Vilma Banky.

Marion's scenario exemplifies the Hollywood tradition of rewriting the ends of plays and novels—e.g., *Love* (1927), a silent version of *Anna Karenina*, *Winterset* (1936), *Our Town* (1940), and *The Glass Menagerie* (1950)—so that they conclude, if not always happily, at least less painfully than they did in their original form. Thus, Kitty does not leave Trent at the end of the movie as she does in the play. Marion shortened the third act so drastically that there was no time for tragedy. She simplified the denouement by reducing it to a series of revelations (Kitty's learning from Shannon that Trent is alive, Trent's futile attempt to conceal his blindness from her) culminating in the lovers' realization that their feelings toward each other had not changed.

In preparing the screenplay, Hellman did not work from Bolton's play (which she claims she never read) but from Marion's adaptation. Although Hellman followed Marion's lead, she nevertheless had a difficult task. First, she had to write a script with dialogue, not a silent scenario with plot points. Then she had to find a cinematic way of conveying the title symbolism. Marion interpreted the title as the angel of death brooding over the battlefield and winging its way to Kitty's home. Hellman found the spectral symbolism pretentious; her angel is a dark presence that is heard rather than seen. The remake of *The Dark Angel* begins with the sound of wind as the credits appear on the screen; it is a sound that recurs at two crucial points in the action—once in the prologue and again at the moment Trent loses his sight. One might even call it a "searching wind," an expression Hellman first heard from a black maid, and which she later used as the title for her fifth play.

Next, Hellman discarded Marion's prologue, in which the lovers repaired to an inn on the eve of Trent's departure for the front. The prologue, which came directly from the play, seemed unrelated to the rest of the action. It was also too theatrical. The mood was predictably ominous; a gypsy shuddered when she read Kitty's

Fredric March and Merle Oberon in *The Dark Angel* (1935), Hellman's first screenplay. *(Samuel Goldwyn Productions)*

palm. Hellman made the inn scene part of the film proper; she also felt it would be dramatically more effective if a bond existed between the three main characters so that, instead of being a conventional tearjerker, *The Dark Angel* would be a film of love and friendship. Having written *The Dark Angel* shortly after *The Children's Hour*, she was still influenced by the triangular structure of her first play, in which the protagonists were two college friends, Karen and Martha, and the male lead was Karen's fiancé. She structured her first script along similar lines, making Gerald Shannon (Herbert Marshall), Alan Trent (Fredric March), and Kitty Vane (Merle Oberon) childhood friends. Then she moved the Shannons next door to the Vanes, made Trent and Shannon cousins, and introduced the trio in a prologue that depicted them as children a decade before the outbreak of World War I. There is still an air of impending tragedy in Hellman's prologue, but it comes from nature. The children are picknicking when a gust of wind scatters their food, prefiguring the winds of war that will blow them apart.

Even in the prologue, Hellman was interweaving the characters' destinies. It was not enough to create one pair of cousins, Trent and Shannon; Hellman added another: Kitty and Laurence, the prissy son of Kitty's Aunt Josephine. Her decision to fashion two sets of cousins from what otherwise would have been four unrelated characters was indicative of her desire to exploit the ironic potential of a plot abounding in chance encounters, sudden revelations, and unexpected discoveries. Both the play and the silent film included a local busybody who happened to spot Trent at the inn and assumed he was there with a girl he had picked up. Hellman made Laurence the busybody, thereby eliminating a superfluous character from the plot and heightening the irony of the situation: the woman Laurence thought was a pickup was his own cousin.

Laurence, who saw Trent taking a tray up to Kitty, kids Trent about his "woman" in front of Shannon. Knowing that Trent and Kitty are engaged, Shannon demands an explanation. Trent refuses. "Think whatever you like," he snaps at Shannon. Later, at the front, when Trent requests a leave to visit Kitty, Shannon, now his commanding officer, refuses, assuming he will use it to see the other woman. Confined to his unit, Trent volunteers for a night raid that leaves him permanently blind. Thus two cousins, one from each household, indirectly cause Trent's blindness: Laurence by his crude joke, Shannon by his refusal to grant Trent a leave. By creating two pairs of cousins, Hellman added to the irony of the plot while at the same time effecting an almost fatalistic interlocking of character and event.

Hellman gave Goldwyn the kind of screenplay he wanted; one in which the action was motivated, the incidents connected, and the plot resolved. It was also the kind of screenplay that could be easily filmed since the filming would be mainly a visualization of the action. For her screenwriting debut, Hellman was fortunate in having Sidney Franklin as director and Gregg Toland as cinematographer. Franklin had distinguished himself at MGM with such films as *Smilin' Through* (1932) and *The Barretts of Wimpole Street* (1933); after *The Dark Angel*, he would make the memorable *The Good Earth* (1937). Toland was already becoming the finest cinematographer of his generation. Together they were able to provide visual and aural links for the narrative connections in Hellman's screenplay, notably by bridging the prologue and the main action as Hellman intended and by juxtaposing Trent's blinding and Kitty's sudden awakening from sleep.

Hellman planned the prologue as a conduit to the main action, into which it would naturally flow. Franklin and Toland facilitated that flow, connecting the prologue with the main action by repeating shots common to both. The prologue opens with a series of dissolves. One shot merges into another; a picture window dissolves into a bed as the viewer is drawn into young Kitty's bedroom on a Saturday morning. She no sooner awakens than she bolts into her grandmother's room, lifts her nightgown unselfconsciously, and warms her backside at the fireplace. The film proper begins ten years later, also with a series of dissolves. The same window dissolves into the same bedroom, and the camera pans slowly over to the bed—the same one we saw in the prologue. A girl awakens; it is Kitty who, although a decade older, still rushes into her grandmother's room and warms herself at the fire.

Another example of cinematic linkage, one that combines both sound and image, occurs when Trent is blinded. A wind blows into the dugout as the camera pans from Shannon, right of frame and looking at a picture, over to the entrance. Shellfire illuminates the picture with a ghostly light. Trent stumbles into the dugout, and a scream is heard. But it is a woman's scream. There is a quick cut to Kitty standing in the hallway of the Vane home as a wind blows through the French doors. Kitty's scream is an early use of overlap, a technique that has become popular with contemporary filmmakers, who often use sound to bridge two scenes by ending the first with a sound that properly belongs at the beginning of the second. In this case, the overlap was also an eerie form of simultaneity, for it seemed that the same wind that howled through the dugout had invaded the Vane home.

There are other impressive cinematic touches in *The Dark Angel:* the gentle passing of time as rain turns into snow that is then melted by the sun; Kitty and Trent turning their backs to the camera to exchange vows; a foxhunt that brings Kitty to the village where the blind Trent is staying; Trent's stunned reaction when he hears her name. Such moments reflect the tastefulness with which the film was made; a tastefulness that carried through to the denouement which, because of Hellman's disciplined writing and Franklin's sensitive direction, never degenerated into bathos.

The silent version, however, was less fortunate. Following the original, Marion set the last scene in Trent's cottage, which became a gathering place for the other characters. First to arrive was Kitty's father who had told Trent what color dress his daughter would be wearing so Kitty would not suspect he was blind. Then Kitty appeared. Their reunion was civilized, and Kitty even accepted Trent's explanation that shellshock made him apathetic to marriage. As she prepared to leave, she extended her hand which Trent naturally did not see. Hurt, she rushed from the parlor but was intercepted by Trent's secretary who told her the truth. Returning, she found Trent pressing his head against a small bust of herself, running his fingers along the contours of the face and weeping.

Hellman had to fashion a denouement from this lachrymose material. However, she felt that the resolution must involve the trio with whom the film began; the father, the bust, and the tears had to go, to be replaced by Shannon, Trent, and Kitty. In order to explain how Shannon knew Trent's whereabouts, she invented the character of Sir George Barton, the head of the hospital in which Trent recuperated. Knowing of Trent's love for Kitty, he phoned Shannon after reading the marriage announcement in the *Tatler*.

Now it is Shannon who infers the truth when Trent fails to take Kitty's hand. It is also Shannon who brings Kitty back into the parlor. Sensing his superfluousness, he withdraws as the couple embrace, and the scene fades out into "The End."

The critics recognized that *The Dark Angel* was a film of quality and not just a "weepie." Encouraged by the reviews that complimented Hellman on her "highly literate" screenplay, Goldwyn purchased the rights to *The Children's Hour*, which was still running on Broadway when *The Dark Angel* went into release in the fall of 1935. However, there was a serious problem with the play: *The Children's Hour* dealt with a student at a girls' boarding school who accused two of her teachers of being lesbians. The Production Code ruled out movies involving "sex perversion or any inference of it."[7] Nevertheless, Goldwyn was interested enough in a movie version to pay $35,000 for the rights to a play so controversial that it was banned in Boston and Chicago, a play whose purchase he could not publicize and whose title he could not use.

There is an apocryphal story that, when Goldwyn was denied permission to use the play's title for the film version because the main characters were presumed to be lesbians, he replied: "We'll make them Americans." Goldwyn may have worn the motley but not on his brain. In his dotage, he would refer to *The Little Foxes* as *The Three Little Foxes*, but in 1935 he was one of the shrewdest producers in the industry. Goldwyn respected Hellman and was pleased with her first screenplay. Thus he believed her when she explained that *The Children's Hour* could be transferred to the screen without violating the Production Code because the play's theme was not lesbianism but calumny. Hellman was correct; it was a nineteenth-century slander case that provided the inspiration for *The Children's Hour*.

2

Ladies in Love: *These Three* and *The Children's Hour*

In 1810, Jane Cumming, a student at a girls' school in Edinburgh, informed her grandmother, Dame Helen Cumming Gordon, that two of her teachers, Marianne Woods and Jane Pirie, who had also founded the institution, displayed an "inordinate affection" in the presence of their pupils. Dame Helen used her influence to have all the students removed from the school and accomplished the task in forty-eight hours. The teachers sued for libel, and despite patently false testimony (Jane swore a maid had observed the teachers embracing through the drawing room's nonexistent keyhole), the jury rendered a four to three verdict in favor of Dame Helen; on appeal, the verdict favored the teachers. But the case was never resolved, and after eleven years the teachers settled for considerably less than the £10,000 they had demanded, each receiving slightly under £1,400. As often happens, the fate of the teachers and their accuser is unknown. But the school in Drumsheugh Gardens never reopened.

Our chief source for the "Great Drumsheugh Case" is William Roughead's *Bad Companions* (1931). It was not the sort of book Lillian Hellman would be likely to read, but it was the kind that would appeal to a writer of detective fiction and former Pinkerton operative like Dashiell Hammett. In the spring of 1933, Hammett told Hellman about the case, suggesting it would make a good play. On 20 November 1934, *The Children's Hour* opened in New York for a run of 691 performances. In the play, Mary Tilford, a student at a New England girls' school, falsely accuses her teachers, Karen Wright and Martha Dobie, of lesbianism. Like Jane Cumming, Mary has an influential and impressionable grandmother, Mrs. Tilford. Like Marianne Woods, Martha Dobie has an actress-aunt,

Lily Mortar, living at the school. And, as one might expect, a nonexistent keyhole is cited as evidence. The teachers sue unsuccessfully for libel. But here life and art diverge. Mrs. Tilford discovers the truth and wishes to make amends. However, it is too late: Karen has lost her fiancé, and Martha has committed suicide.

Some critics have assigned too much importance to Hellman's use of the Roughead book, which Katherine Lederer rightly feels is only of "minor interest."[1] Of major interest is the way Hellman took the main features of the case—the credulous grandmother, the lying student, the actress-aunt, the slip about the keyhole—and incorporated them into a dramatic structure whose foundation is the point where tragedy and melodrama converge. At their juncture is the chance event or the seemingly innocuous object that effects the catastrophe; in *The Children's Hour* it is a bracelet stolen by a student whom Mary threatens with exposure unless she corroborates the accusation against the teachers.

Hellman has taken issue with those who label her plays melodrama, as if melodrama is automatically inferior to tragedy because the fortuitous plays a greater role in the development of the plot. Certainly the most classic of tragedies, *Oedipus Tyrannus*, revolves around a chance event: a meeting at the crossroads where a son unwittingly kills his father. Similarly, an object, Desdemona's handkerchief, is indispensable to the plot of *Othello;* an unexpected delay precipitates the tragedy in *Romeo and Juliet*. Hellman may not have set out to write a classical tragedy; but by choosing a tragic subject and treating it traditionally (forging causal links between the events, building the action to a climax, steering the characters from ignorance to knowledge), she has included most of the elements associated with Aristotelian tragedy.

The Children's Hour exemplifies the classical principle of selection that, according to Aristotle, unifies a work of literature. The writer first chooses a subject and then narrows it down to a theme pervading the entire work. To use Aristotle's example in the *Poetics*, a true epic poet would never attempt to narrate the entire Trojan War or even its main events; rather, the poet would concentrate on a particular feature of it such as the wrath of Achilles, as Homer does in the *Iliad*. Likewise, Hellman is not merely dramatizing a lie; she is dramatizing a child's lie. But it is not a typical childhood lie because Mary Tilford is not a typical child; it is a lie about lesbianism directed against two women who have founded a school in a small Massachusetts town.

Having reduced the lie to a specific allegation, Hellman allows the rest of the drama to evolve concentrically from it, as ripples spread when a pebble is cast into a pool. Here, the pebble is an object, the stolen bracelet mentioned in the opening scene. At first one pays no attention to the disappearance of Helen Burton's bracelet because Helen's role is just a walk-on. But later, when Mary realizes she has erred about the keyhole, she revises her story, claiming it was not she but Rosalie Welles who saw the teachers embracing; and it was on the day Helen's bracelet was reported missing. Rosalie, who stole the bracelet, is afraid of being exposed as a thief; therefore, she cooperates with Mary. A bracelet causes a frightened child to testify against her teachers. Ironically, the bracelet, stolen at the beginning of the play, is recovered at the end.

There is still more irony for Hellman to reveal. Martha no sooner commits suicide than Mrs. Tilford is ringing the doorbell, offering redress. But Hellman is not playing a game with her audience. Dramatists often collapse time so that events that are chronologically discrete seem to occur successively. In *Romeo and Juliet* (act 5, scene 1), Romeo plans to commit suicide because he has not received Friar Laurence's letter; in the next scene, Friar John is explaining to Friar Laurence why the letter could not be delivered. In tragedy, events occur either too soon or too late: Theseus returns to Troezen too late in Euripides' *Hippolytus;* Oedipus arrives at the crossroads too soon; Creon reaches Antigone's tomb too late; Juliet awakens too late; Mrs. Tilford arrives too late. The premature and the belated are staples of tragedy.

Another tragic convention Hellman uses is anagnorisis or self-knowledge. Actually, in *The Children's Hour,* self-knowledge and reversal coincide, much as they do in *Oedipus,* where the protagonist, after learning his origins, rushes off to blind himself. Martha's reaction to the self-knowledge she has acquired is not so different from Oedipus's. Mary's lie forces her to rethink her nature; she concludes that she did harbor an unnatural love for Karen. Martha makes her confession *("I have loved you the way they said")* and leaves the stage. Even before the offstage shot is heard, one knows Martha will not return, just as one knows that when Jocasta exits in *Oedipus* or Eurydice in *Antigone*, it is to take their lives.

There is another similarity between *The Children's Hour* and classical tragedy: the *deus ex machina* ending. Today we tend to think of a *deus ex machina* ending as one that is improbable or forced; a chance resolution like the eleventh-hour reprieve or the sudden arrival of the mortgage money, the serum, or the cavalry. However, most of Euripides' plays ended with a *deus ex machina*, and in the *Poetics* Aristotle called Euripides "the most tragic of poets." In its most basic form, a *deus ex machina* ("god from the machine") involved a god or goddess descending on the scene by means of a crane in order to resolve the action and bring the play to a conclusion. The deity can arrive in time to prevent a catastrophe, as Apollo does in Euripides' *Orestes* just as Hermione is about to be killed and the palace destroyed. Generally, however, the deity arrives after the catastrophe, as Artemis does at the end of *Hippolytus* when the protagonist is dying. Hellman's *deus ex machina* is of the latter kind: Mrs. Tilford appears after Martha has committed suicide.

Generally, an ending requiring outside intervention is considered inferior to one that is internally resolved. However, Aristotle would allow a *deus ex machina* if there were no other way for a character to learn something that was external to the action. In *Hippolytus*, for example, the protagonist cannot tell his father he is innocent of Phaedra's death because he has been sworn to secrecy. Only a deity can impart that information, and so Artemis descends to reveal the truth.

Likewise, in *The Children's Hour*, only a confession from Rosalie would convince Mrs. Tilford that her granddaughter was a liar. But first someone must discover the bracelet Rosalie has stolen; it cannot be one of the main characters, but must be someone on the periphery—Rosalie's mother, who confronts her daughter, learns the truth, and informs Mrs. Tilford.

The Children's Hour was destined to be filmed twice—once in 1936 from Hellman's own screenplay, and again in 1962 from a screenplay by John Michael Hayes. The 1936 version was called *These Three*, although two other titles were considered: *The Hour of*

Liberty and *Women Can Be Wrong*. The 1962 version had the same title as the play; it was also a fairly accurate rendering of the original, containing all the tragic conventions that Hellman had so carefully worked into the plot: the crucial object, the moment of self-knowledge, the *deus ex machina*. *These Three*, filmed at a time when screenwriters had to abide by the Production Code, retained the original premise but rearranged the triangular relationship between the characters so that Martha would not be in love with Karen, but with Karen's fiancé, Joe Cardin. Mary would still make her accusation but it would be one of fornication, not lesbianism.

Ironically, *These Three* was the better film, even though Hellman modified the ending by omitting Martha's suicide and dispensing with the *deus ex machina*. Yet she managed to recreate the spirit of *The Children's Hour* in *These Three* by keeping the play's central theme, the lie that leads to an understanding of the self, and making it meaningful to a mass audience that might not have accepted the idea if it had had lesbian overtones.

These Three was Hellman's first film with director William Wyler, with whom she would work again on *Dead End* (1937) and *The Little Foxes* (1941). It was her second film with Gregg Toland. For the brief period they worked together (1936–41), screenwriter, director, and cinematographer functioned as a team; their common bond was their respect for reality, which each manifested in his or her own way: Hellman by never reducing objective reality to the surreal but selecting only what was representative and universal in life; Toland by deep-focus photography where foreground, midground, and background appeared in sharp focus; Wyler by favoring the long take—a shot longer than the seven-second shot that was customary in the 1930s—over the cut. Wyler was therefore able to film dramatic units instead of fragments and to eliminate unnecessary cutting, which atomized reality. What emerged from the union of "these three" was a form of democratic filmmaking where reality was presented intact, not piecemeal. The distinguished French critic André Bazin noted that Wyler's films were truly democratic because the long takes kept the action from being fragmented and deep focus enabled the viewer to see several planes, not just one.

Hellman invested her screenplay with a similar egalitarianism by dramatizing details that might not require an explanation in the theater but would need clarification in a mass medium like film. A theatergoer would not ordinarily ask how two women happened to start a school, but a moviegoer—at least a 1936 moviegoer—might. Thus *These Three* opens with the women's graduation from college; even the credits evoke commencement time with a scroll-like motif. When Karen (Merle Oberon) and Martha (Miriam Hopkins) return to their dorm after the graduation ceremony, they talk about the future, hoping to find a position together. Karen decides that the house her grandmother left her in Massachusetts would make a perfect girls' school.

Hellman also shows how Karen and Joe Cardin (Joel McCrea) met and how Mary Tilford (Bonita Granville) became one of the first pupils at the Wright-Dobie school. Cardin is at the farmhouse when the women arrive, gathering honey from a bees' nest under the roof. The three become friends, and Joe helps the women renovate the house. While returning with building materials, Joe and Karen encounter Mrs. Tilford, who is looking for a school for Mary. Circumspectly, Mrs. Tilford promises to promote the school on the understanding that her granddaughter will be one of its pupils.

Like the play, in which the lie was deferred to the second act, *These Three* builds gradually to the allegation. The early scenes are idyllic, even romantic: Karen reclining on a pile of two-by-fours in a wagon that moves lazily along a country road; Karen and Joe sipping a soda, lovers' style—two straws in one glass; Joe's proposal to Karen on a carousel at a local fair. The classes seem relaxed and orderly until one day a bracelet disappears, and Rosalie Welles is seen concealing it in her desk during Latin. Now the action can never return to its tranquil beginning.

Although the bracelet will cause Rosalie to commit perjury, the circumstances will be different because Hellman has altered the nature of the accusation and the accuser. In the film, Mary is a malcontent who lies out of boredom and frustration. Since she expected her grandmother to provide her with a private tutor, she would be unhappy at any school. When her elders cater to her, which means not reprimanding her for lying, she is relatively harmless; but when she is exposed as a liar, as she is on three occasions

Joel McCrea, flanked by Miriam Hopkins *(left)* and Merle Oberon, in *These Three* (1936), Hellman's screen adaptation of *The Children's Hour*. (Samuel Goldwyn Productions)

(for using a pony, for taking credit for a bouquet of flowers that really came from the garbage can, for faking a heart attack), she retaliates by punishing her accusers. In the play, Mary was a child Iago who doted on *Mademoiselle de Maupin*, Gautier's novel about a transvestite heroine, from which she learned enough about aberrant sex to make her charge believable. In fact, one could imagine the role interpreted in such a way as to suggest that Mary was a latent lesbian herself, particularly since she enjoys playing knight and forcing the other girls to take oaths of fealty to her. But in the film, Mary, as portrayed by Bonita Granville, seems ignorant of sex; it is as if hatred has sapped her sexuality. And her attempts at vassalage are just adolescent dreams of conquest originating in narcissism, not lesbianism.

Mary of *The Children's Hour* knew enough about lesbianism to convince her grandmother she was telling the truth. Mary of *These*

Three knows only what she sees and what she infers. Once Martha, Karen, and Joe penetrate her facade, she fabricates a lie out of impression and conjecture to punish them. Hellman and Wyler show exactly how Mary obtained her data.

One evening, while waiting for Karen, Joe falls asleep in Martha's room. When he awakens, he accidentally knocks over a glass. There is a quick cut to Mary who is awakened by the sound. She slips into the hallway just as Martha begins picking up the pieces of broken glass. But the sound also awakened Martha's aunt, Mrs. Mortar, who reminds her niece that Karen and Joe will be marrying in the spring. Saddened by the thought of losing her friend, Martha weeps as Mary looks on from the shadows, having witnessed Joe's leaving Martha's room and Martha's tears over Karen's forthcoming marriage.

Although there is no reference at all to lesbianism in *These Three*, it seems as if everyone associated with the production, including composer Alfred Newman, knew the subject matter of the original and tried to suggest it. The score contains a motif that might be called "Martha's Theme"; it is plangent, not oozy, but it lacks the hopeful, romantic character of the music associated with Karen and Joe. "Martha's Theme" is often heard when the women are together; in fact, we hear it when they arrive at Lancet and see the farmhouse. Interestingly, we hear it again when Martha glances over at the sleeping Joe. It is a moment of intense loneliness. The camera pans from Martha, watching him doze off, over to the window and back to Martha. The music accompanying the pan shot seems to suggest that Martha is lonely because she is losing Karen to Joe, not because she is losing Joe to Karen. Axel Madsen is correct when he writes that "Miriam Hopkins acts as if her desire is for her companion and not the man whom Merle Oberon loves."[2] However, Martha's suppressed love for Karen exists within the subtext of the film; it is something one senses rather than perceives. The text is the same as it was in the play—the ironic repercussions of a lie.

One of the key scenes in the play occurs when Mrs. Mortar accuses Martha of harboring an "unnatural" love for Karen. For the film, all Hellman had to do was alter a few lines and change the gender of the pronouns so that the accusation would reflect

Martha's love for Joe rather than for Karen. As a result, Mrs. Mortar's dialogue required little emendation. "Don't think you're fooling me, young lady" can be said to a woman in love with a man or with another woman; "I should have known enough to stay out of your way when *he's* here" (which is substantially what Mrs. Mortar says in the play) can mean that Martha is irritable because she is losing her friend to a man or because she is losing a man to her friend. Of course, Hellman had to omit "unnatural"; instead, Mary alludes to what is "going on." Yet Mary can still say, "They've got secrets, funny secrets," and the line can be as effective on the screen as it was on the stage. Actually, Hellman's changes were few in the allegation scene. Since it is now Martha's room that figures in the testimony, it is Martha who says, "There is no keyhole on my door," which was Karen's line in the play.

Although Mary will err about the keyhole, she is cleverer in the film than she was in the play, where she seemed to be living on the fringe of literature, playacting at being the definitive villainess. The Mary of *These Three* is not well read; she would hardly know enough French to get past the first paragraph of *Mademoiselle de Maupin*. As she demonstrated in Latin class, languages were not her forte. But she makes up in cunning what she lacks in learning. Mary knows how to capitalize on a stroke of luck. After hearing that Rosalie caught her arm in the door when she was eavesdropping, Mary rips off a piece of the girl's petticoat and twists it around her upper arm so there will be visible proof of Karen's "cruelty." By now, Rosalie is Mary's vassal; earlier, Mary had intimidated the girl into giving her money—a slight change from the original, in which Mary browbeat another student. By making Rosalie the victim of Mary's shakedown, Hellman enhances the film's credibility; Rosalie has already been preyed upon and forced to take "the worst oath there is." A threat of imprisonment breaks her spirit completely; she will now swear to anything. Such incidents ring true, for most of us have witnessed the tyranny of the unregenerate.

Since *These Three* will not end tragically, or at least not as tragically as *The Children's Hour*, Hellman can keep the trio intact until the denouement. Again, she just had to revise some of the original dialogue. In the play, Joe reminds Mrs. Tilford of the "two people" who have come before her "with their lives spread on the table"; in the film, it is "three people." Since Joe is now implicated in the lie, he asks Mary if she were telling the "exact truth about us," not the "exact truth about Miss Wright and Miss Dobie" as he says in the play.

Wyler's compositions also maintain the sense of a united trio in the confrontation scene with Mrs. Tilford. He begins the sequence by framing the three characters in the doorway and repeats the three-shot during the sequence to indicate their solidarity. At the end of the sequence, Wyler fades out on the trio in a state of shock and dissolves to a long shot of the courtroom where the judge dismisses the slander suit.

For the conclusion, Hellman was able to use three incidents from the last act of her play: the closing of the school, Joe's dismissal from the hospital, and the unmasking of Mary through the discovery of the bracelet. Wyler was able to duplicate the stark opening of the third act, where the women sit alone in an empty house, with a shot of Karen and Martha by the fire; slowly the camera pulls away from them, revealing a window streaked with rain. Significantly, "Martha's Theme" is heard softly in the background.

Having altered the nature of the original charge, Hellman must now change Martha's confession from loving a woman to loving a man. Again, the emendations are not substantial; they consist primarily of reassigning dialogue. In *The Children's Hour*, Joe asks Karen if she and Martha were lovers; in *These Three*, Karen asks Joe if he and Martha were lovers:

The Children's Hour

KAREN: Ask it now.
JOE: Is it—was it ever—
KAREN: No. Martha and I have never touched each other.

These Three

JOE: Say it now. Ask it now.
KAREN: I've nothing to ask. All right. Were you and Martha ever—
JOE: Karen, Martha and I never even thought of each other.

In both play and film, Karen sends Joe away, but for different reasons. In the play, he leaves because Karen insists they need time apart; in the film, he leaves because Karen still has doubts. When Martha asks why he has gone, Karen does not reply as she did in the play ("He thought that we had been lovers") but says instead: "Because I told him I thought that you—and he—" Then "Martha's Theme" is heard. Karen is midway on the staircase, Martha at the foot of the stairs. Martha's "I do love you" of *The Children's Hour* becomes "I do love him." Her wrenching "Maybe it's been there since I first knew you" becomes "I think I loved him the first day we came here."

These Three will also be resolved through the recovery of the bracelet. However, since Hellman has modified the original ending, it will not be Mrs. Tilford who calls on Karen, but Martha who calls on Mrs. Tilford. Mulling over some comments her aunt made about the bracelet's disappearance, Martha seeks out Rosalie, who finally admits the truth. Mary has kept the bracelet, presumably to blackmail Rosalie if she ever weakened, and the housekeeper discovers it in Mary's bureau.

Now play and film diverge. Martha does not want Mrs. Tilford to feel remorse as Karen did in the play. Instead, she makes Mrs. Tilford her messenger, instructing her to contact Karen and tell her to "go to Joe, wherever he is." Since Joe is in Vienna, Karen finds him in a Viennese coffeehouse, where they embrace to the music of the love theme played in waltz time.

Although love triumphs at the fade-out, an air of sadness lingers on because one feels Martha's absence. The film had centered on a trio, and now one member has withdrawn from it. Because Hopkins played the scene with Mrs. Tilford nobly and without the sniffles of self-pity, one does not ask what she does or where she goes. Martha simply steps aside so that these three can become those two. The main difference, then, between *The Children's Hour* and *These Three* is not the shift of genders, the reallocation of dialogue, or even the change in the nature of the charge. Rather, it is the reduction of a trio to a couple *(These Three)* as opposed to the atomization of a trio into a solitary person *(The Children's Hour)*. For the couple, there is hope; hence the optimistic although not necessarily happy ending of *These Three*. For the solitary, there is bleakness; hence the unrelievedly stark conclusion of *The Children's Hour*.

A quarter of a century after *These Three*, Wyler would be able to film *The Children's Hour* as Hellman had written it. In 1960, homosexuality was still a screen taboo, although, like most taboos, it could be broken by filmmakers who knew the difference between suggestion and depiction. An aura of homosexuality hung over *Suddenly, Last Summer* (1959), and a brace of 1960 Oscar Wilde films, *Oscar Wilde* and *The Trials of Oscar Wilde*, neither concealed nor portrayed their subject's sexual preference. The very year Wyler was preparing to film *The Children's Hour*, *Victim* (1961) was released, a British film (with Dirk Bogarde) attacking Britain's discriminatory laws that made homosexuals easy prey for blackmailers.

Such films, however, were the exception rather than the rule. The rule was *Tea and Sympathy* (1956), in which a prep school student, mistakenly thought to be homosexual in the play, is derided as "sister boy" in the movie. Wyler and United Artists did not anticipate an easy time and were willing to release the film without the Production Code seal if necessary. As it happened, the code was revised in 1961 "to allow homosexuality and other sexual aberrations as subjects . . . *after* several major companies had gone into production with large-budget films dealing, at least in part, with homosexuality—*Advise and Consent*, *The Children's Hour*, and *The Best Man*."[3] However, despite the code revision, *The Children's Hour* was neither a critical nor a commercial success.

Perhaps it would have fared better if Hellman had written the screenplay as she had planned. In 1960, Hellman met with Wyler in Rome to work on the script. Unfortunately, she had to withdraw from the project; Hammett's death in 1961 caused her to lose interest in it. The adaptation she did gave her screen credit, but the actual script was written by John Michael Hayes, who originally entitled his version *The Infamous*, then just *Infamous*, no doubt in imitation of those provocative one-word titles of the 1930s (*Reckless, Dangerous, Desirable, Illicit*).

One doubts that even a catchy title would have helped much. Still, the film is worth discussing because of what it reveals about screenwriters who are too respectful of the works they are adapting.

Hayes was not a novice; he had written the screenplays of Hitchcock's *Rear Window* (1954), *To Catch a Thief* (1955), and *The Man Who Knew Too Much* (1956). One can imagine the frustration he must have experienced in trying to be faithful to Hellman and to himself. A screenwriter will want to leave his or her mark on the script, even if it is an adaptation. When Hayes deviates from Hellman, it is generally for the worse. Perhaps, and this is conjecture, the film might have had a greater impact if Hayes had attempted to answer the question many theatergoers have always had about Mary: Is she, in fact, the repressed lesbian of the drama? Is Mary, who reads *Mademoiselle de Maupin* and prefers to play the knight rather than the lady, psychologically akin to the headmaster in *Tea and Sympathy* who accuses a student of what he fears in himself?

Unfortunately, Hayes weakened the role of Mary. His Mary does not read Gautier, only pulp novels that elicit "Wow!" and "Double wow!" from the other girls. She does not think in terms of knights and vassals, but in terms of sororities and sisters. Thus she forces Rosalie to take an oath not to betray a "fellow sister."

One might also question whether Wyler was the right director. As he later admitted, it was difficult for the director of *These Three* to make *The Children's Hour:* "I still remembered what I had *not* been able to do in the old picture."[4] He also remembered what he had done. Influenced by memories, he tried to duplicate the rhythm of the earlier film by opening on an idyllic note. The credits appear as the girls bicycle across a bridge. The camera tracks up the path to the school, where a concert is in progress—the concert being the equivalent of the commencement in *These Three*. Just as the graduation served to introduce Mrs. Mortar, so does the concert. Lily Mortar is now a faded grande dame, played by Miriam Hopkins, the Martha of *These Three*, and played surprisingly well, with a hint of a Southern accent to soften the character's selfishness.

Since the film follows the play fairly closely, Wyler makes it clear from the outset that Martha has adopted the masculine role in her relationship with Karen. Quite early in the film, Martha (Shirley MacLaine) recalls her first impressions of Karen (Audrey Hepburn) when they were at college: "What a pretty girl!" MacLaine managed to convert her pixie ways into boyishness and turn her usual ebullience into self-effacement; she became a familiar type, the plain jane with bobbed hair who willingly stands in her friend's shadow as long as her place is not usurped by a man. Martha idolizes Karen, thinking of her in terms of a fashion model who must always be "kept up" in the latest styles. Like the play, the film conveys the tension existing between Martha and Joe (James Garner), here the typical bachelor who is always stopping by for a free meal. When he shows up for dinner, Martha curtly remarks that he should pay tuition. When he tries to apologize for his callousness, Martha rebuffs him: "Damn you! Leave me alone." The line is not quite so strong as the play's "God damn you," but the sentiment is the same.

At least the film stresses the fact that Martha and Karen are intelligent women with a genuine interest in culture—an interest Joe does not share. When Karen remarks that after marriage they can read books together, Joe affects a feminine voice and mocks her, not the way a man would ridicule a woman but the way a male who thinks the arts are for the effete would ridicule another male who believes they are for everyone. By emphasizing Joe's boorishness, Hayes was only bringing out what was latent to begin with; he did not add a new dimension to the character. No one, in fact, seems to have added much. Even Alex North's score evokes *These Three*. There is a new "Martha's Theme," first heard during the credits and again while Martha is walking in the school grounds alone. Like her theme in the previous film, it is the violins' reduction of loneliness to plangency. Mary also has a leitmotif—"Skip to My Lou" played in a minor key, jangling and dissonant.

Thus there is a double context for the 1962 *Children's Hour:* the original play and *These Three*. Wyler and Hayes keep referring to both. Just as the sound of a falling glass awakened Mary in *These Three*, the sound of a falling iron awakens her in *The Children's Hour*. Martha is ironing as she berates Karen for being more interested in marriage than in the school. In her anger, she drops the iron; Wyler cuts directly to Mary bolting from her sleep as he did in the earlier film. She slips into the hall just in time to see Karen leaving Martha's room. In a long shot, Karen stands left of frame; Mary is right of frame behind a partially closed door that diagonally divides her face, suggesting a schizoid nature. The composition is arresting but misleading. This Mary is not schizoid; she is just a spoiled child who will do anything to get out of attending school.

This Mary, played abominably by Karen Balkin, is also not very intelligent. She has to be told what "unnatural" means, the crucial word in the accusation. When the girls who overheard the argument between Martha and her aunt repeat the word Mrs. Mortar had used about her niece, Mary is puzzled by its meaning. In the play, it was Peggy who asked what "unnatural" meant. However, Mary does know that the word irks her grandmother. The film transfers the famous whisper scene from the living room to the limousine that is bringing Mary back to the school. When she sees the "school zone" sign from the car window, she speeds up the tale, whispering the conclusion in her grandmother's ear. The whisper was sufficient in the play and in *These Three*; but Hayes, apparently thinking the charge had to be substantiated, had Mrs. Tilford ask Mrs. Mortar if she ever used the word "unnatural" about her niece. "The whole thing's unnatural," Mrs. Mortar exclaims, meaning Martha's jealousy of Joe. It is then that Mrs. Tilford prevails upon her friends to withdraw their daughters from the school.

For the confrontation between the women and Mrs. Tilford, Wyler cannot repeat the compositions he used in *These Three*. Since Hayes's script follows the play, the shots must emphasize separateness rather than solidarity. When Mary enters the parlor, she sits in a chair in the background, with Joe in front of her, Mrs. Tilford left of frame, Karen right, and Martha center. When Rosalie appears, the trio splits into three separate figures: Martha left, Karen center, and Joe right. After Rosalie corroborates the lie, Wyler evokes a feeling of polarization as Karen, left of frame, rests her head on Joe's shoulder while Martha stands by herself on the right.

Visually, the confrontation is effective; dramatically, it lacks the power it had in *These Three* where admissions were followed by denials and accusations by rebuttals. Hayes retained much of Hellman's dialogue, reassigning some lines and omitting others. For some reason it is Martha, not Karen, who now says, "The wicked very young, and the wicked very old." Hayes obviously knew *These Three*, for Joe still refers to the "three people" who have come before Mrs. Tilford, as he did in the 1936 film, rather than the "two people" as he did in the play. Since the accusation no longer involves Joe, it would have made more sense to use the original line. Hellman could switch dialogue, skip lines, and connect ellipses; Hayes could not without leaving gaps and fissures in the dramatic framework.

In adapting the third act, Hayes made two changes, one minor but fitting, the other significant but anticlimactic. The minor change involved Martha's manner of suicide; she now hangs, rather than shoots, herself. The change enabled Wyler to break loose from the script and do something visually exciting. As Karen goes out for a walk, Martha watches her from the bedroom window; then the curtains suddenly close. Karen's walk in the school grounds recalls the one Martha took earlier in the film. Then it was one lonely woman walking by herself; now it is another. "Martha's Theme" begins softly; then it turns dissonant, rising to a cacophonous crescendo as Karen, sensing something is wrong, rushes back to the house and breaks down the door to Martha's room. One sees only the vestiges of the suicide: an overturned chair and dangling feet in silhouette.

The second and more radical change was structural. In the original, the revelation occurs after Martha confesses her love for Karen and commits suicide; in the film, it occurs after Martha's confession but before her suicide. Martha is now present when Mrs. Tilford arrives, offering to make restitution. But Martha has already admitted the truth about herself and cannot live with it. No public apology can restore the ignorance of self that made life bearable for her. Martha's presence at a disclosure that was originally meant to follow her death robs the scene of its irony and makes her suicide a gratuitous action or a gesture of defeat. One cannot say, "If only Martha had heard the truth!" because she did hear it.

Since Hayes reversed Hellman's order of events, the film could not end the way the play did—with a repentant Mrs. Tilford calling on an unforgiving Karen. Instead, it ends with Martha's funeral.

The moment of truth as Martha (Shirley MacLaine) admits her love for Karen (Audrey Hepburn) in *The Children's Hour* (1962), John Michael Hayes's adaptation of Hellman's play. *(United Artists)*

Karen delivers a quiet eulogy; picking a flower from a bouquet, she places it on the coffin. "Good-bye, Martha," she whispers. "I'll miss you in my heart." Oblivious to Joe and Mrs. Mortar, who stand at the graveside, she proceeds down the road, her walk becoming a stride. Karen is no longer the stylish creature who has to be "kept up" in the latest fashions. She is wearing flats, an ill-fitting cloth coat, and a beret. The camera tracks in for a close-up of a face that has grown mannish, or more charitably, androgynous—but clearly no longer elfin.

Here, then, is the film's one original contribution to its source: the possibility that Karen may also be a lesbian. It is an intriguing notion, but one is simply not prepared for it because Hepburn's Karen was so completely feminine. For the ending to be plausible, Hepburn would have had to suggest a homoerotic side to the character early in the film, as MacLaine had done. Since the suggestion is never made, there is no cumulative evidence for Karen's metamorphosis. Thus the film concludes with a hypothesis instead of culminating with a disclosure.

Hellman was her own best adapter, as she showed in *These Three*. It seems that *The Children's Hour* will reveal its secrets only to its author; to others, it behaves like a silent oracle.

Dockside in Hollywood: *Dead End*

Before attempting to adapt *The Children's Hour*, John Michael Hayes might have analyzed the way Hellman adapted a major play for the screen—Sidney Kingsley's 1935 Broadway success, *Dead End*. The 1937 film version reunited Hellman with Wyler and Toland; it was also her third screenplay for Goldwyn. Goldwyn, Wyler, and Hellman had agreed on a faithful adaptation, and so she set about restructuring the play to make it work as a film.

First, Hellman had to explain to moviegoers why the action was set on a stretch of dockside by New York's East River where a luxury apartment house faced a slum. Kingsley intended the setting as a metaphor for urban inequity and underscored his thesis with an epigraph from Thomas Paine: "The contrast of affluence and wretchedness is like dead and living bodies chained together." Hellman replaced the literary epigraph with a simple printed prologue that began by stating that "Every street in New York ends in a river"; the prologue then went on to explain that the rich, in their desire to have riverview homes, pushed eastward until they reached a dead end and the ultimate urban paradox—"apartments that looked down on the windows of tenements."

Wyler's camera immediately responded to the prologue by visualizing its thesis. In an unbroken crane shot, the camera descends the face of an apartment house, tracking left across tenement roofs and alighting at the entrance of a quayside apartment building whose residents can lunch on the terrace and watch the slum children swimming in the river. The shot has made its point, and the screenplay enlarges upon it.

Hellman favors leisurely beginnings; she prefers to define character and setting rather than jolt the audience into attention as Kingsley did. In the play, the curtain no sooner went up with an

"Aw ta hell wid yu" than a Jewish boy, who had recently moved into the neighborhood, was being "cockalized." Hellman will use the initiation ceremony, which consists of rubbing dirt into the genitals of the circumcised newcomer, but not at the outset; and given the strictures of the Production Code, not on camera. She is more concerned with establishing the milieu from which the five "Dead End" kids come: the tubercular T.B., the slow-witted Dippy, the incorrigible Angel, Spit the punk, and Tommy the scrapper. She also wanted to explain that it was not friendship but clannishness that kept the five of them together. Thus she established their insularity in the opening scene. "Get a load of that," Spit says contemptuously at the sight of Milty, the Jewish boy.

Restructuring the play was not so difficult since Kingsley wrote short vignettelike scenes resembling set pieces, which could easily be rearranged. Hellman's real problem was Kingsley's symbolism, which she could not discard but which she had to temper so that a drama of slum dwellers, street gangs, syphilitic prostitutes, and washed-up hoods would not turn into a Brechtian parable. For all its street-smart dialogue, *Dead End* is a curiously literary play, abounding in antitheses. The setting is a social interface, with the East River Terrace Apartments fronting a row of tenements. The women are diametric opposites: Kay, who wants luxury so badly that she becomes a millionaire's mistress to get it; Drina, who wants a better life for herself and her brother Tommy and will go out on strike to achieve it. The male leads, Gimpty and Martin, are a familiar duo: the boyhood friends whose lives take them in opposite directions. Gimpty becomes an architect; Martin, a criminal. Even the play's informers are paired: Gimpty, the adult betrayer, and Spit, his teenage counterpart. Gimpty informs on Martin; Spit names Tommy, one of his own gang, as the assailant of a prominent businessman.

Another literary touch is the water imagery that recurs throughout the play. The water is contaminated literally and metaphorically; unlike the archetypal river, the East River has no regenerative effect. The boys swim in polluted waters; Kay embarks on a yacht trip that will take her into moral servitude. Gimpty remembers how, as a boy, he guarded the matchbook boats his friends sailed in the gutter, trying to keep them from "going into the black hole of the sewer." Significantly, he delivers this speech as Kay is about to journey into the black hole of materialism with her millionaire lover.

Hellman could convert Kingsley's antitheses into sets of contrasting characters who would be identifiable types (the kept woman, the working woman, the slum boy who turned to the professions, the slum boy who turned to crime) instead of embodiments of the author's social views. But Kingsley's proletarian poetry would have to go. And Gimpty, the proletarian poet, would have to speak in prose. However, before Hellman could deflate Gimpty's rhetoric, she had to simplify his character. The architect is nicknamed Gimpty because "gimp" is slang for cripple; his real name is Pete.

Kingsley had a reason for making the architect a cripple: Gimpty's disability shows that slum life ravages the body as well as the spirit. Furthermore, a leg crippled by rickets gives one the right to attack an environment that leaves men with withered limbs. Thus Gimpty's passionate speeches are understandable in terms of his physical affliction as well as his crusading spirit. But Hellman did not want a philosopher-hero who could deliver a Darwinian sermon about the God that Mother Evolution planted in the hearts of men; nor did she want a Jeremiah cursing the Empire State Building as "the biggest tombstone in the world." She wanted a doer, and 1937 moviegoers wanted a romantic hero who was not a cripple. With Joel McCrea slated to play the architect, the name of Gimpty would have to go, and with it the withered leg; his new name is Dave, and he walks tall.

Changing Gimpty into Dave affected the characterizations of Drina, Kay, and "Baby Face" Martin. In the play, Drina is in love with Gimpty, who, until the very end, is oblivious to her virtues. For most of the play, Gimpty pursues Kay, who returns his love as best she can—by sleeping with him occasionally. In the original, Kay's role was bigger than Drina's; but not in the film. Hellman's sympathies are with Drina. In the play, Drina made her first appearance when she came to Milty's aid as he was being cockalized. In the film, Drina first appears in a scene with her brother Tommy that emphasizes her desire to get him out of the slums, even if it means risking a policeman's club to walk on a picket line.

There were several reasons why Hellman built up Drina's role at the expense of Kay's. First, Sylvia Sidney, who had been cast as Drina, was a bigger star than Wendy Barrie, who had been signed for Kay. Hellman also understood strikers like Drina. In 1936, the year before she started the *Dead End* screenplay, Hellman's second play, *Days to Come,* was produced; it dramatized the effect of a strike on an Ohio factory town. The year 1937, when *Dead End* was released, was a year of strikes, 4,720 in all, eighty-two percent of which were settled in favor of the unions. And just as *Dead End* went before the cameras, Chicago police were responsible for the death of ten Republic Steel strikers and the wounding of over ninety others. Most important of all, Hellman was involved in unionism herself; following the passage of the National Labor Relations Act in 1935, Hellman actively supported the Screen Writers Guild's struggle to become the sole bargaining agent for writers.

To strengthen Drina's role, Hellman pared Kay's to the bone, making her a breezy, good-natured gold digger, tired of being "hard up" and willing to sell herself for security. Hellman's Kay is more interested in Dave than he is in her; Dave only dates her when Drina is unavailable. Kay is also shallower in the film. She enjoys slumming with Dave, euphemistically referring to their dates as opportunities to enjoy the "free things" New York has to offer.

Hellman also robbed Kay of her only virtue—humanity. Kingsley's Kay would occasionally slip out of her luxury apartment to spend the night with Gimpty in his hovel. Hellman's Kay sees a cockroach climbing the wall of Dave's tenement and flees down the stairs. Whatever sympathy Hellman took from Kay she gave to Drina, even going so far as to add a poignant scene in which Drina recounts a childhood fantasy about falling ill on the subway and being helped by a kindly gentleman who brings her to his house in the country.

In the play, it almost seems as if Gimpty wins Drina on the rebound. In fact, Drina keeps complaining that Gimpty ignores her. But in the film, Drina and Dave have a common goal: a better life—Drina for her brother, Dave for humankind. However, Kay is interested in the easy life, not the better one. Thus Dave tells Kay almost paternally that she does not belong in his world, nor he in

Sylvia Sidney and Joel McCrea, the proletarian and the architect, in *Dead End* (1937), Hellman's adaptation of Sidney Kingsley's play. *(Samuel Goldwyn Productions)*

hers; in the play, Gimpty groveled before Kay, begging her not to leave on her lover's yacht.

Having changed Gimpty into Dave, Hellman also had to change the architect's relationship with the gangster, "Baby Face" Martin (Humphrey Bogart). Kingsley's Martin was not unsympathetic; he was a gangster who had lost his charisma and could only look good by doing knife tricks for naive kids. Kingsley's Martin proves the thesis that slums breed criminals, a point Gimpty makes when he calls Martin a decent person destroyed by his environment. It is Martin who experiences the reversal of fortune found in tragedy. Like a tragic protagonist, he suffers rejection, disillusionment, and betrayal in a single day: his mother disowns him, his old girl friend turns out to be a disease-ridden streetwalker, and Gimpty informs on him.

Hellman's Martin is an enemy of society, not a victim of his environment, and hardly a tragic figure. Just as she stripped Kay of her humanity, so she discourages sympathy for Martin, chiefly by not having the architect inform on him. In the movies, the romantic lead is not an informer. But more important, Dave has no reason to betray Martin; Gimpty has.

In the play, Martin ridiculed the architect. When Gimpty admonished him for teaching the boys about gang warfare, the boys scoffed at Gimpty "who angry but impotent walks away." Later, during an argument, Martin stomped on his crippled foot. "Just wait!" Gimpty cries, prophetically. Thus Gimpty's reasons for betraying Martin to the police was not entirely to rid the neighborhood of a menace; he also wanted satisfaction for the public humiliation he received.

In the film, Dave has not suffered any indignities from Martin. It is only when Martin tries to kill him that the architect retaliates, pursuing the gangster across the roofs and shooting him as he clings to a fire escape. That Martin should come crashing down from a tenement fire escape is an ironic reminder of his own attempt to escape poverty through crime, only to meet his death in the neighborhood he thought he had left behind. Martin's fall is also a striking example of Hellman's ability to wed action and symbol.

A comparison of the play and the film enhances one's respect for

Hellman as an adapter. Because she followed the general outlines of Kingsley's plot, the reviewers believed she had produced a literal transcription of the original. Yet by additions, deletions, and subtle shifts of emphasis, she was able to make the play less of a street poem and more of a street drama so it would be accessible to a mass audience. Admittedly, it is difficult for one writer to be faithful to another as well as to oneself. Hellman's chief virtue as an adapter was her ability to be faithful to her source without compromising her own art. Therefore, she retained the play's key scenes and much of the original dialogue. But there were times when the dialogue would not work as Kingsley had written it. In such cases, she retained what she could. Often she would start with the first line of a scene, skip a section, and pick up the rest later, connecting the beginning and end of the ellipsis as if she were making wires meet.

For example, in the sequence in which Martin sees his old girl friend, Francey, Hellman naturally omits their earthy memories of teenage sex, but she does not skirt the fact that Francey has syphilis. In the play, Francey specifically tells Martin not to kiss her on the mouth. In the film, a simple "no" sufices, as Francey, played with a washed-out fatalism by Claire Trevor, turns sharply away from him. When Martin begs her to come with him, she defiantly stands in the light, crying, "I'm tired, I'm sick." Hellman can now cut Martin's next line in the play ("What's a matter wid yuh?") since he has obviously *seen* what the matter is, and segue into "Why didncha get a job?"

Hellman had the advantage of seeing her adaptation brought to the screen by two artists who shared her view of realism: Wyler and Toland. Toland's cinematography often achieves the effect of portraiture. One shot is justly admired for its Rembrandt-like quality: the low-key shot of Martin and his mother on the stairs of the tenement, their faces appearing out of a background of total darkness. The film's visual style is not at odds with Kingsley's play, which was an attempt to blend realism and naturalism. Wyler and Toland achieved that blend by shooting faces through the bars of fire escapes to suggest a prisonlike environment and by using deep-focus shots to include poverty and affluence in the same frame. The boys are frequently seen on the dock in the foreground with the doorman at the luxury apartment in the background.

At the end, the film's visual art comes full circle as the camera reverses its opening movements—this time ascending rather than descending. Wyler took his cue from Kingsley. The play ends as the doorman douses the fire the boys have started. It is a symbolic act, but it does not have the effect the doorman intends: he cannot "dampen their spirits." Instead, the boys gaze at the smoke spiraling into the sky with a combination of awe and nostalgia. Their spirits rise, if only for a moment, for there is no rising up through the ranks for them. Dolefully, they begin singing "If I Had The Wings Of An Angel" as the curtain falls. At the end of the film, the camera tracks the boys as they move along the quay into the night, singing the same song. Then, suddenly, the camera begins to crane up past the tenements and into the sky, with the upward mobility the boys will never know.

4

Beasts in the Parlor, Whelps in the Woods: *The Little Foxes* and *Another Part of the Forest*

Hellman's third—and last—collaboration with Wyler and Toland was the screen version of her most popular play, *The Little Foxes*, which opened on Broadway in 1939 and became a film in 1941. *The Little Foxes* introduced a family that is as much a part of the American theater as the Days of Howard Lindsay and Russel Crouse's *Life with Father* (1939) or the Lomans of Arthur Miller's *Death of a Salesman* (1949): the Hubbards of Alabama, who, as the play opens, are wooing a Northern financier to back their cotton mill, which they expect will make them the equal of New England dynasts. The family includes the patriarchal Ben Hubbard; his sister Regina Giddens, her husband Horace, and their daughter Alexandra, usually called Zan; Oscar, the brother of Ben and Regina, his wife Birdie, and their son Leo.

Hellman wrote her own screenplay for *The Little Foxes;*[1] it represented a return to the type of screenplay she had written for *The Dark Angel:* a prologue of short scenes followed by a series of longer ones—microdramas, or sequences with their own beginning-middle-end unity, that reproduced the film's structure in miniature. It was true screenwriting as opposed to dramaturgy, as a comparison of stage and screen versions makes clear. In her play, Hellman built the first act on a series of alternating rhythms—a slow, even rhythm for exposition, a faster one for plot advancement. The curtain rose on a conversation between the Hubbard domestics, Addie and Caleb. Their exchange establishes the fact that the Hubbards and their guest of the evening, the Chicago industrialist Mr. Marshall, are just finishing dinner.

When Birdie Hubbard flutters in, rhapsodizing about Mr. Marshall's love of culture, the stage rhythm matches her effusiveness. A reprimand from her husband puts an end to her prattle, and one rhythm—the rhythm of nervous enthusiasm—is exchanged for another—that of after-dinner talk: genteel, overly decorous, and, in this instance, rippling with undercurrents of self-satisfaction. A business transaction has just been concluded; the Hubbards have succeeded in getting Marshall's backing for their mill. Hellman uses multiple rhythms for the after-dinner scene in the play: the false graciousness of small talk; the ooze of rhetoric that coats the platitudes and pleasantries; the repressed euphoria of people trying simultaneously to conceal their glee and observe the amenities.

However, Ben Hubbard cannot sustain the pose. When Marshall mistakenly calls the nouveaux riches Hubbards "aristocrats," Ben corrects him with oily politeness. Now the pace accelerates as Ben, proud of his common origins, narrates the rise of the Hubbards in a parable of conquest, contrasting Birdie's family—plantation owners who could not adapt to the postbellum South—with his own merchant-class people. The parable builds to a climax, culminating in a boast: "Twenty years ago we took over their land, their cotton, and their daughter." With its conclusion, the rhythm ebbs into an embarrassed pause as Birdie looks down in humiliation, after hearing herself described as a chattel. Hellman balances Ben's insensitivity with a compassionate gesture from Marshall: "May I bring you a glass of port, Mrs. Hubbard?"

With his gentlemanly offer, one dramatic segment ends and another begins; and with it, another set of rhythms. For the rest of Act 1, Hellman uses the contrapuntal rhythm of manipulation, of pressure and acquiescence, of give and take, of demand and trade-off, as Oscar and Ben prevail upon their sister to get Horace Giddens to put up his share of the money for the mill. However, Horace, a cardiac invalid, is currently at Johns Hopkins hospital. Regina will have her husband brought back from Baltimore if Ben raises her share of the profits; Ben agrees, but to raise Regina's, he must reduce Oscar's. Oscar shrilly objects, but Ben throws his brother a sop by intimating marriage between Zan and Oscar's son, Leo. Hellman keeps alternating between exultation and degradation, triumph and defeat. Birdie, the first main character to appear, is the last to leave. She entered with ebullience; she exits in humiliation after Oscar slaps her across the face for warning Zan that she may be forced to marry Leo. When Zan hears Birdie's cry, Birdie, suppressing her pain and grief, says stoically, "It was only my ankle." And the curtain falls on the first act.

Hellman knew exactly how much of Act 1 could be transferred to the screen. But first the title had to be explained. The title came from a passage in the Song of Solomon (2:15) that also served as the play's epigraph: "Take us the foxes, the little foxes, that spoil the vines, for our vines have tender grapes." Although Horace speaks the same verses in the film, the epigraph was presumably considered too erudite to introduce the movie. Instead, a simple introduction followed the credits: "Little foxes have lived in all times, in all places. This family happened to live in the deep South in 1900."

Next, Hellman had to rework the beginning. The play's opening scene was uncinematic; it was stage exposition, the familiar "dusting off the furniture" in which the domestics functioned as an expository prologue. In its place, Hellman substituted a cinematic prologue: the morning of the dinner party. A Southern mill town slowly comes to life. A horse ambles up a country road, pulling a wagon full of cotton with a black farm hand lying peacefully on the bales. Clothes are washed outdoors, cotton is unloaded at the warehouse, and a buggy moving at an even pace brings Addie and Zan back to the Giddens house with provisions for the dinner.

A filmic rhythm has been substituted for a stage rhythm, a rhythm of images for a rhythm of language; in this case, images of backwoods innocence. Wyler connected these vignettes with dissolves and wipes as one shot blended into another or wafted it away. It is a lazy morning; the clan has not yet awakened.

When it does, Hellman introduces the members to us. As the buggy pulls up the pathway, Birdie calls down to Zan, eager to rehearse the Schubert they will play after dinner. Regina stands imperiously on her second-story porch; Ben appears at the window, complaining of the music. The foxes have their own rhythm; it starts slowly but accelerates when the machinations begin. However, breakfast is not a time for duplicity. Regina and Zan take their morning coffee under the portico in one of Gregg Toland's pictorial deep-focus shots depicting background and foreground with equal clarity. Beyond the portico, a gardener is hoeing; in the background is a white picket fence, and beyond it, a cluster of trees.

The pace quickens as the business day begins. Slow dissolves cannot capture the transition from morning ease to bustling activity. Thus Wyler decides to cut from one action to another. He cuts from Zan and Regina at breakfast to David Hewitt, the liberal editor who did not appear in the play but was added as the love interest for Zan,[2] looking out of his window as Leo Hubbard strides self-importantly into his uncle's bank and Ben saunters along to the warehouse, jauntily swinging his walking stick. Then Wyler cuts back to the Giddens house, where Regina is clipping roses and Addie is washing Zan's hair. "The dinner will go fine tonight," Addie notes reassuringly, and in the next shot, the dinner is about to conclude.

Having found the right way to open the film, Hellman was able to adhere to the plot and preserve a good deal of the original dialogue. Sometimes she had to change a word ("nigger" becomes "darkie") or shorten a sentence; sometimes she had to restage a scene or shift lines when she discovered that dialogue that might not fit one context would fit another. For example, Ben still delivers his attack on the flabby Southern aristocracy, ending with the same boast. But now he delivers it at the dinner table, a factor that intensifies Birdie's embarrassment. Naturally, Marshall cannot ask Birdie if she would like some port, since it will not be served until they retire to the drawing room. Consequently, Hellman had to transpose some dialogue. Originally, Regina rebuked her brother for boring Marshall with "ancient family tales" after Marshall offered Birdie the port. Now Regina reprimands him after his demeaning speech. Yet someone should console Birdie; if not Marshall, then another character. In the film, it is Addie. Hellman took one of Addie's lines from the beginning of Act 1—"You look pretty this evening and young"—and had Addie deliver it after Birdie's humiliation. Birdie can even answer as she did in the play: "Me, young?" Her reply is actually more poignant than it was on stage, for it comes after an incident that would make any woman feel her age.

By having Addie console Birdie, Hellman makes Marshall less sympathetic than he was in the play; now he is just a financier interested in making money from the Hubbards. However, there was another reason why Hellman made Addie Birdie's comforter: it was part of her attempt to humanize the blacks in the film so that they would be more than domestics entrusted with the exposition. As a child in New Orleans, Hellman had a warm affection for her black nurse, Sophronia, a name that appears in several of the plays. Thus Hellman added another scene in the film to reveal more of Addie's charitable nature. When some hungry black children peer into the kitchen, Addie tells the cook to feed them, recalling Christ's command to feed the hungry but confessing that she does not exactly know where Christ said it.

The Hubbards, on the other hand, practice their own form of Christianity. There is a wonderfully ironic moment in the play (which does not occur in the film) when Marshall commends the Hubbards on following Christ's teachings. What he has unwittingly described is an inverted Christianity in which the Hubbards do unto others what they expect others to do unto them; only they do it first.

Hellman has always claimed that the Hubbards of the play were meant to be humorous; and they are—grimly so. However, the celluloid Hubbards are not humorous. On the stage, they had an operatic flamboyance that Hellman toned down for the movie, with a corresponding loss of gusto. Leo Hubbard in the film is simply obtuse. Dan Duryea, who would later create some interesting screen villains, played Leo as a clod instead of the dapper parvenu he really was. Bette Davis was never happy with the role of Regina. She played it well but without the self-parody that its creator, Tallulah Bankhead, brought to it. Bankhead had the ability to step out of the character from time to time, as if she were stepping out into the alley for a cigarette, and laugh at Regina's excesses. Any actress playing Regina should be able to laugh at Regina's villainy without laughing at Regina; a difficult task, to be sure, and one that only a star who is both a personality and an artist can accomplish.

Hellman realized that characters who were bigger than life on the stage would, on the screen, resemble overweight children in tight-fitting clothes. Accordingly, she scaled the Hubbards down to the size of the rectangular screen, making them recognizable types who gained in universality what they lost in bravura; and in Regina, Hellman created a perennial type—a woman who must face the fact that she is aging.

Regina of the movie is not a Southern Circe; she is a middle-aged woman who hears the footfalls of time all too distinctly. At one point, Regina compares an oval photo of herself as a young woman with her reflection in a mirror. Before Horace returns, she makes herself up carefully, studying her face as if it were a map. These scenes, which were not in the original, succeed in being moving because Regina has appeared at her most vulnerable—at her mirror.

Whether Hellman was adding new scenes or merely adapting her play, Wyler saw to it that what she had written reached the screen with no diminution of power. His task was facilitated by the screenplay, which duplicated the original three-act structure and the way each act came to a natural conclusion. Wyler would have to devise a cinematic equivalent for the end of each act. The end of Act 1, when Birdie warns Zan about Ben's marriage plans for her, is especially tricky. On the stage, Oscar would stand in the doorway and overhear his wife's conversation with Zan. Then Zan would climb the stairs to her bedroom, and Birdie would move toward the doorway. When she reached it, Oscar would slap her across the face. Zan must then rush down the stairs, stopping midway when Birdie feebly explains that she has twisted her ankle.

In the theater, the scene must be staged so that one movement balances another. As Zan ascends the stairs, Birdie must start walking cautiously toward her husband. Any deviation in the timing—an upstage cross executed too early or begun too late—would weaken the dramatic impact. Unlike a stage director, Wyler was not limited to the Giddens drawing room, the play's only set. With a larger playing area, he can have Birdie take Zan aside at the living room entrance-way that is framed by tie-back drapes. Oscar, left of frame, is in the hallway, partially hidden by one of the drapes so he can eavesdrop more realistically than he could on stage. When he strikes Birdie, Zan rushes out on the landing, calling down to Birdie, who replies as she did in the play. However, the film's first act does not end with the departure of Oscar and Birdie. Caleb then enters the drawing room and extinguishes the candles as the scene fades out. The tranquil ending is in sharp contrast to the duplicity and tension that marked the earlier part of the evening. The first act has come full circle; it began on a peaceful note and concludes on one. Yet it is a bogus tranquillity, for it is merely a lull between battles.

The play's second act included a narrated incident, Zan's overnight stay in Mobile with her father, which Hellman dramatized for the film in an attempt to enlarge Zan's role and strengthen her character. Realizing that her ailing father cannot travel home nonstop from Maryland, Zan breaks the trip at Mobile, where she not only demands accomodations on the first floor of their hotel, thus inconveniencing some of the guests, but also gives the headwaiter detailed instructions about the menu. Zan of the film is hardly an ingenue, despite Teresa Wright's natural winsomeness, which is often cloying. In fact, the hotel clerk notes that Zan is exactly like her mother.

Hellman envisioned *The Little Foxes* as the first play in a trilogy about the Hubbards; she never realized her intention, although she did write a companion play, *Another Part of the Forest* (1946), that portrayed the Hubbards in 1880, twenty years before the time of *The Little Foxes*. It is interesting to speculate on the kind of woman Zan would have been in the third play. Hellman was thinking of making her an embittered spinster earning her living as a social worker! If O'Neill's *Mourning Becomes Electra* (1931) is any indication of the interlocking patterns that exist in a family, then the children will end up resembling whatever parent they hated, just as Christine Mannon in the O'Neill trilogy turns into the mother she loathed and Orin becomes more like his father. At the end of *The Little Foxes*, when Zan becomes her mother's tormentor by refusing to spend the night with her, Ben observes that Zan is getting to be "right interesting." Apparently he senses a fox in the making, "interesting" being the highest compliment he can pay to his own kind.

The scene in Mobile reveals an aspect of Zan's personality that does not come through in the play—a domineering quality she shares with her mother. One wonders if Hellman would have developed that tendency in the hypothetical third play or if she were already thinking of Zan as a younger Regina when she was writing the Mobile scene for the screenplay.

The notion of parent and child as twin reflectors is seen—literally—in another episode that occurs in the play but not in the same setting: the second act conversation between Oscar and Leo about Horace's Union Pacific bonds. Hellman repeats the dialogue almost verbatim, but for the film she transferred the scene from the drawing room to the bathroom where father and son converse while shaving. Visually, the effect is mesmerizing. The men are shaving back to back—Leo in a circular mirror, Oscar in a rectangular one. The result is a double reflection. It is almost surreal yet optically valid: a mirror offers a reverse image. However, part of Oscar's image is reflected in Leo's mirror, and part of Leo's in Oscar's. Father intrudes on son, son on father. Leo will become what Oscar is, just as Oscar was once what Leo is.

The screenplay's second act offers further proof that Hellman understood that what worked on the stage might not work on film. The pivotal object in both play and film is Horace's medicine bottle that breaks in the third act just as he is having his heart attack. Naturally, the audience must be made aware of its importance early in the plot. In the play, as Zan unpacks the medicine, she speaks one of those lines that telegraph calamity: "Careful Addie, it must not break." Hence it is not a question of wondering if it will break, but when. However, this is a stage line, too fraught with dramatic foreshadowing to sound natural on the screen. Hellman rewrote the line to make it sound less portentous. Zan simply unpacks the medicine, murmuring a quick "Careful, Addie" and noting that there are two bottles—one for downstairs, another for the bedroom. Therefore, when the bottle breaks in the living room and Horace asks Regina to fetch the other one, the existence of a second bottle does not come as a surprise.

In film, it is not enough just to allude to a medicine bottle; it must become a visual presence, not merely a verbal reference. In a shot that recalls a similar one in *Citizen Kane* (1941), the bottle appears left of frame on a night table next to Horace's bed; on the same table are a glass and a pitcher of water. In itself, the shot may seem insignificant. However, what is significant is that Toland

William Wyler (1902–1981) directing Bette Davis and Teresa Wright in
The Little Foxes **(1941). *(Samuel Goldwyn Productions)***

photographed *The Little Foxes* after he finished *Citizen Kane*. One
shot in *Kane* particularly impressed André Bazin: the deep-focus
shot that followed Susan's suicide attempt. We do not see her
attempt suicide after her fiasco as an opera singer. A stage light
goes out, and in the next shot, one sees a night table, left of frame,
with a glass and an empty pill bottle; in the background is the door
through which Kane rushes. Toland clearly repeated the *Kane* shot
in *The Little Foxes*. Although it is often difficult to determine a
cinematographer's specific contribution to a film, the deep-focus
shots in *The Little Foxes*, especially the one of the medicine bottle
on the night table, bear the Gregg Toland signature.

The Little Foxes also bears Wyler's signature. It is a typical
Wyler production for several reasons: it illustrates the director's
ability to film a play without its becoming photographed theater; it
typifies his preference for long takes that encompass greater detail

than normal shots; and it reflects his tendency to create visual parallels between contrasting scenes, often by staging them within the same setting or in similar settings.

In *The Little Foxes*, visual parallelism is the most obvious feature of Wyler's art. Consider the scene in which Oscar, Leo, and Ben discuss Horace's bonds, which they plan to "borrow" so they will not be dependent upon the Giddens money for their business venture. Wyler stages the scene in the living room entrance-way with Leo flanked by his uncle and father. The men fill the frame with their bulk; the archway cannot accomodate the three of them, so they hover conspiratorially in front of it. One cannot help but recall an earlier scene in which a secret conversation also took place in the entrance-way. Then, however, the shot was more symmetrical because it included only two characters, and slender ones at that: Birdie and Zan.

Parallelism even appears in the way in which each of the film's three acts ends—with a visual coda reinforcing the curtain line. The film's first act had the same closing dialogue as the play ("I only twisted my ankle") but included a scene without dialogue to round it out: Caleb's extinguishing the candles. Similarly, the film's second act ends with the same dialogue that brought the curtain down on Act 2: Zan crying "Don't listen" as Regina taunts Horace with the prospect of imminent death. The film's second act, however, continues beyond the dialogue. Wyler dissolves from Zan embracing her father to Leo's face reflected in the brass plaque of Horace's bank; obviously he is there to "borrow" the bonds. The dissolve cushioned the blow of the earlier scene in which Regina told her husband, "I hope you die." In each act of the film, including the third, which will be discussed shortly, the curtain line, taken directly from the play, is followed by a wordless scene that brings it to a truly cinematic conclusion.

Like the play's third act, the film's opens in deceptive tranquillity. Zan is in a crab apple tree, and David lies on the grass. The unthreatening mood continues with an album-type shot of the five stalwarts, the only decent characters in the film: David, Horace, Zan, Addie, and Birdie. The shot recalls an earlier group portrait, one darker in tone and malevolent in design—the Hubbards and Marshall, the foxes and their prey in their parlor-lair.

Hellman repeats virtually all of Act 3's opening dialogue, including Birdie's speech about elderberry wine curing hiccups. There are, however, two significant additions that deflect the action from the idyllic path it seems to be taking. Hellman has Horace deliver the play's epigraph in a meditative manner, as if he had found a biblical parallel between the foxes who spoil the vine and the Hubbards who despoil the South. She also has a slightly tipsy Birdie disclose her true feelings about Leo: "I don't like Leo, my very own son." Significantly, in the movie version of *Another Part of the Forest*, Lavinia Hubbard will say the same about all her children—Regina, Oscar, and Ben.

The most powerful scene in both play and film is Horace's heart attack in the final act. Hellman builds to it slowly, with a glacial exchange between Regina and Horace. When Regina reminds her husband to stay out of her part of the house, Horace applies the Hubbards' first law: punish the other before the other can punish you; or, in this case, its amendment: punish the other because the other has punished you. Horace informs Regina that he knows about the bonds but will take no action, thereby rendering her powerless. Regina retaliates with the Hubbards' second law: one bad turn deserves a worse one. She destroys whatever is left of Horace's masculine pride by confessing that she found him so repellent that she deceived him into thinking her health was too delicate for sex. At this point Horace, completely demoralized, suffers his attack, reaching for the medicine bottle so quickly that he knocks it over.

In the screenplay, Hellman omitted Regina's boast that she cheated her husband of his marital rights. She did so, first out of deference to the Breen office which was in charge of administering the Production Code and which miraculously overlooked the fact that Regina was never punished for causing her husband's death; and secondly because the boast would only have been meaningful in terms of an earlier reference to Horace's "fancy women" that Hellman had also deleted. However, the scene has a thrilling theatricality without the taunt. Regina enters, looking thoroughly predatory in her bird-crowned hat with the veil drawn tightly across her face like a net. She stands by the window as the rain cascades down the panes. It is there that she tells Horace why she married him: because she had resigned herself to what she would *not* be getting out of life. Horace is sitting left of frame; Regina crosses over to him and sinks into an arm chair, right of frame. When the bottle falls to the floor, Regina remains immobile, her pursed lips conspiring with her stony and dispassionate eyes as she affects the look of a bystander who conveniently ignores an act of violence by staring straight ahead.

Wyler and Toland reportedly had difficulty deciding how to shoot the scene, yet Hellman's stage directions were so explicit that a filmmaker had only to translate them into cinema: "Regina has not turned during his climb up the stairs." Wyler ended up doing exactly what Hellman had prescribed: he kept the camera on Regina during the entire scene. Her face dominates the frame, never going out of focus; it is Horace who goes out of focus as he staggers out of the drawing room and makes his painful ascent up the stairs. It is only when he collapses on the staircase that Regina calls for help.

With Horace's death, Regina can regain her power over her brothers. Seated regally in the same arm chair from which she witnessed her husband's heart attack, she dictates her terms to Ben and Oscar: 75 percent of the business or exposure for the theft of the bonds. Again, Wyler simply follows Hellman's stage directions: "Alexandra comes slowly down the steps." In a magnificent deep-focus shot, Oscar and Ben are left of frame; Regina right; and Leo center. Alexandra begins her descent as Regina threatens the trio with jail. Unperturbed by her daughter's presence, she finishes her speech and dismisses the men.

The only real defect in the play is Ben's third act peroration, which reduces the drama's theme to a thesis: "There are hundreds of Hubbards sitting in rooms like this throughout the country." Hellman omitted the line in the screenplay. The opening title about little foxes living "in all times, in all places" was sufficient. Yet Hellman retained Ben's exit line in which he called Zan "right interesting." Ben knows a Hubbard when he sees one, and although Zan may have her father's surname, she is her mother's daughter, as the Mobile hotel clerk noted. Each Hubbard is the other's fury; kinship is the link between transgression and retribution. In a universe where there are no deities to exact vengeance, humans must execute the will of the gods. Zan is now her mother's prosecutor, but a prosecutor with a social conscience who sees her family not as nouveaux riches but as scourges of society, scavengers who eat the earth, or to use the imagery of the epigraph, who spoil the vine. Zan refuses to be a passive witness to such devastation.

Wyler stages the final scene between mother and daughter on the staircase, certainly one of the most dramatic of settings as well as one of the most archetypal, recalling as it does the *scala* or stairs that the quester climbs to meet his fate. When Regina asks Zan to spend the night with her, she is standing midway on the stairs; Zan is at the foot. The composition is the reverse of an earlier staircase scene, the one in which Regina cursed Horace. There, Zan was on the second-story landing.

As Regina makes her request, the camera pans over to the bedroom door behind which Horace's body lies. Thus Zan's final line, "Are you afraid, Mama?", which is also the play's last line, is even more pointed. Although the play ends with Zan's taunting question, the film goes one step further, concluding the way the first two acts did: with a visual coda rounding out the drama. Zan rushes off into the night, and from her bedroom window, Regina sees her daughter and David making their way through the downpour. The final shot is of Regina at the window as the rain streaks the panes. A film of tears coats her eyes, but Regina is not weeping. Rather, her eyes glisten with self-pity and the realization that the fate to which she was born, loneliness, is now hers. Wyler expresses that loneliness by a slow fade as Regina's face darkens into a silhouette.

Generally, Wyler realized Hellman's intentions. However, in certain matters determined by Goldwyn or his aides, any director or screenwriter would be powerless. One doubts whether Wyler or Hellman had anything to do with the way the credits were designed. Despite Hellman's attempt to make the blacks more than stereotypical darkies, the magnolia tree credits along with Meredith Wilson's score of recycled spirituals evoke the plantation society of *Gone with the Wind*. When "The End" appears on the screen, an unseen chorus breaks into an "Alleluia" as if the blacks whom the Hubbards had exploited were rejoicing over Regina's fate.

Even Hellman fell victim to her own liberal sentiments when she had David observe that the whites may know the dances but the blacks have the rhythm. In the post–civil rights era, such a statement has the ring of racial condescension, however unintended.

But these are minor blemishes: the film can still be called a successful screen adaptation. Of course, no film can or should replicate the original; it can be better, worse, or different from it. David Lean's *Great Expectations* (1946) is not Charles Dickens's; it is more graceful, more poetic than the novel. Similarly, the bravura manner in which the Hubbards practice villainy is absent in the film. The reason is that the Hubbards are a stage family; they are like figures in a nineteenth-century melodrama who connive flamboyantly and speak with a slimy grandiloquence. They are the underside of the Days of *Life with Father*, but no less American. One is fascinated by the civility with which they topple each other, never allowing the heat of anger to dry up their oily rhetoric. The stage Hubbards evoke the founding fathers whose grim portraits adorn the walls of local museums. Wyler could not duplicate their villainous grandeur, for it would look artificial on the screen. Since film is a more realistic medium than the theater, the Hubbards are even deadlier in the movie; they are also more believable than they were on the stage because they have lost their theatrical quaintness.

What Wyler and Toland did achieve was the filmic equivalent of Hellman's lean, taut prose through compositions of austere monochrome; in *The Little Foxes*, power and corruption are not painted in strong, vibrant colors but seem to be sketched in India ink by a hand that can trace the lineaments of evil.

The play premiered in February 1939; the movie version in late summer 1941. The sequel, *Another Part of the Forest*, opened on Broadway in November 1946; the film was released in the spring of 1948. *Another Part of the Forest* was not the Broadway hit *The Little Foxes* was, although it made a star of Patricia Neal, who created the role of the young Regina. The film version was impressive despite the fact that it was not produced by a major studio. Universal-International bought the rights to *Another Part of the Forest* for $250,000, a rather high price for a studio that was not one of the big five (i.e., RKO, Paramount, Warner Brothers, Twentieth Century—Fox, and MGM). In 1946, Universal merged operations with International Pictures to form Universal-International. In the early and middle 1940s, Universal's specialty was sand and sex sagas with Maria Montez, Sabu, and Jon Hall; monster movies featuring the Wolf Man, Dracula, Frankenstein, and the Mummy; Abbott and Costello comedies; and mini-musicals with Donald O'Connor and Peggy Ryan. Occasionally, Universal would produce a quality film (the 1943 remake of *The Phantom of the Opera;* Hitchcock's *Saboteur,* 1942), but for the most part, Universal's films of the World War II period were programmers, movies that occupied the second half of double bills.

Once Universal became Universal-International, it attempted to produce more quality films, wooing stars like Ronald Colman for *A Double Life* (1948) and Edward G. Robinson for the movie version of Arthur Miller's *All My Sons* (1948). It also signed the eminent stage couple, Fredric March and Florence Eldridge, for two films: *An Act of Murder* (1948), a powerful movie about euthanasia marred only by the ending, and *Another Part of the Forest.* The films were shot back to back; both starred the Marches, and both were directed by Michael Gordon, certainly one of the most under-rated directors in the industry. Gordon had a genuine gift for the theatrical, which undoubtedly derived from his stage experience. He excelled at thrillers like *The Web* (1947) and *Woman in Hiding* (1949) and brooding melodramas like *The Secret of Convict Lake* (1951).

Gordon had an outstanding cast to work with. In addition to the Marches, who would play Marcus and Lavinia Hubbard, Ann Blyth, who had scored a success a few years earlier as Joan Crawford's incorrigible daughter in *Mildred Pierce* (1945), was signed for Regina. Dan Duryea, who played Leo in the stage and screen versions of *The Little Foxes,* would appear as Oscar—an interesting case of an actor playing members of different generations, just as Miriam Hopkins played Martha in *These Three* and Martha's aunt in *The Children's Hour.* Edmond O'Brien, who had worked for Gordon in *The Web* and was costarring in *An Act of Murder,* took on the role of Ben Hubbard.

The screenwriter was Russian-born, Sorbonne-educated Vladimir Pozner. In the 1930s, Pozner worked in the engineering department of MGM in France and then became general manager of MGM International Films Corporation. He returned to the Soviet Union in the 1950s, where he worked as a reporter until he became the Voice of Moscow, disseminating propaganda in perfect English for Radio Moscow. Gordon remembers that even in the late 1940s Pozner had a good command of English and a "sense of screenplay structure that was sound and inventive—a talent we were most in need of."[3] The combined talents of cast, director, and screenwriter resulted in a film that *Time* magazine called "a nearly perfect example of how to film a play."

Given the title, which derives from a stage direction in several Shakespearean plays, 1948 moviegoers might have expected a forest; and a forest is what they saw at the outset. However, it is not a decorative forest, but a functional one. The credits begin with a tracking shot of woods illuminated by shafts of sunlight. As the credits continue, it is apparent that the camera is not just roaming the woods but accompanying someone. At first, it is hard to determine who it is; but as the credits end, the figure hurrying along the path becomes distinct: it is a woman with a bouquet of flowers in her arms. Soon she will have a name—Lavinia Hubbard. She stands on the bluff overlooking the site of a Confederate training camp, now a square with a monument commemorating the young men whose camp was overrun by Union soldiers in the spring of 1864. It is Confederate Day, and the people of Bowdon have gathered to honor the youths who died when someone betrayed the location of their camp.

It is a compelling opening, for it immediately focuses the viewer's attention on the massacre, the attitude of the townspeople toward the Hubbards, and the reason for Lavinia's leaving the bouquet at the base of the monument when everyone has left the square. Clearly there is some connection between the Hubbards and the fatal night in 1864. As Colonel Isham finishes his eulogy with a reference to the raid, the camera swish pans up the hill where Lavinia stands, wearing the face of tragedy, as if she had overheard him.

Frankly, the film has a more effective opening than the play, in which there is no reference to the raid until the third act. As drama, *Another Part of the Forest* is less satisfying than *The Little*

Foxes because Hellman seems more interested in mythic ideas than in structure; the Hubbards of the sequel inhabit a southern Olympus where they behave like Homeric deities, conspiring against and supplanting each other. Brooding over the play, like an ancestral curse, is the sin of Marcus Hubbard; it was he who was responsible for the massacre.

Another reason why, as a play, *Another Part of the Forest* lacks the tautness of its predecessor is that Hellman was trying to show what the Hubbards were like in 1880, twenty years before they spoiled the vine. Before Regina was Mrs. Horace Giddens, she was a Hubbard—selfish but not yet lethal. Hellman opened the play with a rendezvous between Regina and John Bagtry, Birdie's cousin, who knew happiness only during the Civil War and who now wants to fight in Brazil to preserve the institution of slavery. Regina loves Bagtry, but he does not return her love. The Bagtrys are in love with their dreams; they cling to their plantation, Lionnet, but are neither strong enough to maintain it nor clever enough to borrow on it.

The Hubbards, on the other hand, are both strong and clever. They covet Lionnet, but to acquire it, Regina must marry the wealthy banker, Horace Giddens; and Oscar, who is infatuated with the local whore Laurette, must marry Birdie. A familiarity with *Another Part of the Forest* might make one more sympathetic to Regina and Oscar as they appear in *The Little Foxes*, especially when one realizes that neither married a chosen spouse.

Although Hellman could assume that theatergoers would make the necessary connections between the two Hubbard plays, Pozner could not assume the same of moviegoers. Thus he treated *Another Part of the Forest* as an independent work, adapting it according to the cardinal principle of screenwriting: he planted clues early in the film by stating what the crime was, referring to it periodically, and explaining it at the end. The crime hovers over the action. It is even present on Lavinia's birthday, which happens to coincide with Confederate Day, the one day she refuses to use salt. Her abstinence is not a form of eccentricity; it is her way of atoning for what happened sixteen years ago when Marcus ran a Yankee blockade to buy salt, which he then sold for the outrageous price of $8.00 a bag. On that same night, someone led the Union troops to the training camp.

Pozner could not begin as Hellman did, with the Regina-Bagtry meeting; it would not be sufficiently dramatic and would involve too much exposition. Instead, he made the meeting the second sequence, deferring it until the Confederate Day ceremony had ended. However, the rendezvous follows the ceremony in point of narrative, not in point of time. Film can create its own temporal and spatial relationships by intercutting several events so that they will be taking place simultaneously, not successively. The result is irony of a special kind. Three Hubbards are in the same general area at the same time, each unaware of the other's presence. Lavinia is watching the memorial service high on a hill; Oscar is attending the service with Laurette, much to the annoyance of the townspeople; and in "another part of the forest," Reginia is meeting John Bagtry.

In addition to rearranging some episodes, Pozner made other changes in the plot to make it acceptable to a mass audience. His most signficant change involved Lavinia; both he and Gordon agreed that she could no longer be the neurotic she was in the play (where she was really Birdie of *The Little Foxes* grown addled); instead, she must appear the victim of the Hubbards' greed. Unlike her husband, who is what he has done, Lavinia is what she has seen. Unable to bear that vision, she has withdrawn into herself and her dream of building a hospital (in the play, a school for black children) to atone for Marcus's sin. There is a good deal of dark humor in the play that is absent in the film, as it would have to be, once Lavinia is transformed from an eccentric into a scapegoat.

To humanize Lavinia, Pozner had to dehumanize the other Hubbards, who emerge as a family of rotters, unable to behave decently even at Lavinia's birthday party. When Lavinia begins to cry, Marcus snaps: "Stop crying over your food if you want it to remain unsalted"—a line that does not appear in the original and is another illustration of Pozner's way of keeping Marcus's "old sin" before the audience. The line acquires deeper significance from the juxtaposition of two seemingly unrelated images that turn out to have a common bond. As Marcus and Regina go off to their part of the forest to read Aristotle, Lavinia knocks over a salt shaker. A shot of the salt trickling from the overturned shaker dissolves to one of Regina's parasol, which Marcus is twirling as if it were a toy. The dissolve mocks the meaning of Confederate Day and trivializes Lavinia's birthday party; it also clarifies Marcus's main interests: Regina, on whom he dotes, and the classics, which he can afford to read in expensive editions because during the Civil War he cornered the market in salt. But the associations do not end there. Gordon suddenly cuts from Marcus and Regina as she reads Aristotle on the nature of happiness, to a happy couple: Oscar kissing Laurette. The cut is jarring; the juxtaposition of father/daughter, man/woman is so quick that the connection is inevitable: Oscar is doing to Laurette what Marcus would like to do to Regina.

Hellman has made this connection possible, for an air of unconsummated incest hangs over *Another Part of the Forest*. It is even intimated in *The Little Foxes* when Regina raises a mild objection to Leo's marrying Zan because they are first cousins. When Oscar reminds Regina that their grandparents were also first cousins, she replies: "And look at us." One might also look at Marcus Hubbard, who is jealous of his daughter's infatuation with John Bagtry. What Regina has found in Bagtry is a younger version of her father. In the play, Bagtry is 16 years older than Regina; in the film, Pozner had to omit the age difference since Ann Blyth and John Dall were about 20 when the movie was being made. Still, he managed to retain the play's incestuous atmosphere in the scenes between Regina and Marcus and in the conclusion as well. Knowing where the power in the family now resides, Regina adopts the same air of adolescent sensuousness that she used on her father and saunters over to her brother Ben.

Inevitably, Pozner would have to dramatize narrated material as Hellman did in her *Little Foxes* screenplay. One such incident that could not be shown on stage was the Klansmen's attack on Sam Taylor, a Northern financier who was planning to give the Bagtrys a loan on Lionnet. By intercutting the attack with a cancan at the Cairo Gardens, Gordon created a visually exciting sequence. As the night riders closed in on Taylor, Gordon cut back to the Cairo Gardens where Laurette was leading the cancan. Shots of kicking legs alternated with white-robed men on horseback. A horse neighs in the darkness while Taylor stands defenseless on a bridge; Laurette does a split at the very moment Taylor falls to his knees, beaten by the riders.

Gordon also tried to reproduce as much of the stage action as he could in the film. Thus, except for a few scenes, he confined most of the action to the interior of the Hubbard house or the side portico. To give the illusion of a real house, Gordon showed the Hubbards in various parts of it as Wyler had done in *The Little Foxes*. In one shot, Marcus is on the patio talking up to Ben on the upper porch as Regina looks out the window. Gordon was also able to film two crucial scenes—the second act climax and Ben's third act discovery of his father's crime—so that they had the wholeness of stage action without appearing stagy.

In movies, the staircase has always been the perfect setting for murder (*Frenchman's Creek*, 1944; *The Strange Love of Martha Ivers*, 1946; *The Spiral Staircase*, 1946) or intended violence (*The Curse of the Cat People*, 1944). Gordon uses the staircase for a special kind of horror, the kind families create when they turn a household into a battlefield. Marcus is on his way to bed when he turns midway on the stairs and faces Oscar, who is pleading for money so he can marry Laurette. Ben is at the foot of the stairs. The argument attracts Regina, who appears below, as well as Lavinia, who comes out of her room and stands at the top of the stairs. A perfect composition results, with the Hubbards stationed as if they were marshaled for war. By staging the altercation on the staircase, Gordon could balance a cry from above with a shout from below, building the scene to a thunder and lightning climax.

The scene itself is a series of accusations and reprisals. When Ben scoffs at his brother for pining over a floozy, Oscar pulls a gun on him. Marcus rushes down in a combined state of rage and terror. Ben, suspecting his father's implication in the massacre, asks Marcus why he is frightened of a pistol. To thwart her brother's plan to marry her off to Horace Giddens, Regina informs her father that Ben increased the amount of the loan the Bagtrys requested for Lionnet. In turn, Ben reveals Regina's infatuation with John Bagtry. Enraged, Marcus strikes Ben, ordering him to leave the house

Ben Hubbard (Edmond O'Brien) clashes with his father Marcus (Fredric March) while Lavinia (Florence Eldridge) tries to intervene in *Another Part of the Forest* (1948). *(MCA Publishing)*

the next morning. For a fitting climax, the camera tracks up the stairs to a window lit by lightning, as Lavinia collapses on the landing.

Gordon was equally successful with the third act confrontation between Marcus and Ben, also staging it on a staircase, but this time outdoors—on the steps leading to the upper porch. In the play, Lavinia's reasons for telling Ben about his father's connection with the massacre were complex. Marcus reneged on his promise to build her the school and had also threatened to commit her to a mental institution. In the film, Lavinia makes the disclosure because Marcus has banished his son. Lavinia begins her story as Marcus walks up the steps to his room. Once Ben learns the facts—which, incidentally, are clearer in the film, where there is no doubt that Marcus led the Union troops to the Confederate camp and was not just followed by them—he demands that his father sell him the store for a dollar and sign over all of his assets. Ordered to his room like a child, Marcus slowly ascends the stairs.

Gordon's handling of the final scene is a textbook illustration of converting theater into film. The scene involves three playing areas: the outside stairs, the portico, and the breakfast table on the patio. When Marcus goes up to his room, Ben takes his father's place at the breakfast table. When Marcus returns, he sits alone on the portico, next to the coffee table. To convey a totally loveless atmosphere, Pozner ignored Hellman's stage direction calling for Regina to pour her father some coffee, but not to sit with him. In the film, Regina does neither. Disregarding her father's request for coffee, she crosses the patio to join her brother.

Pozner even made a further change in the final scene to show the Hubbard children as morally worthless. The original ended with Lavinia's bidding farewell to her children in a semimad scene, as if she had wandered into the last act of *Lucia di Lammermoor* and decided to imitate the heroine's lyrical raving. She has a memento for each of her children; for Ben, she has a watch. What Ben really wants is the Bible in which Lavinia recorded the details of Marcus's involvement in the massacre. Lavinia compromises and offers to will it to him.

Since Pozner never intended to make the Bible part of the plot, he had to rewrite Hellman's ending. But he had another reason for ending the screenplay the way he did: his Lavinia is not daft; she is a sensitive woman haunted by the past. In the play, Lavinia never expressed her feelings for her vulpine brood; in the film, she speaks her mind with quiet candor: "It seems funny to say, but I don't like you, Benjamin. I don't like any of my children." With that, she ascends the outside stairs, and, in a stunning crane shot, the camera joins her, both of them transcending what is on the ground below: Marcus alone on the portico and the children at the table, all looking dwarfed as Lavinia rises above them.

Despite the left-wing backgrounds of both the screenwriter and the director, *Another Part of the Forest* never degenerated into an anticapitalist tirade or Marxist propaganda. Pozner, who had coauthored the screenplay for the anti-Nazi film *The Conspirators*

(1944), did not allow his political convictions to interfere with his characterization of Lavinia, however tempting it might have been to portray her as a victim of capitalist exploitation.

Gordon's political background is well documented. In his 1952 testimony before the House Committee on Un-American Activities, Elia Kazan included Gordon among the members of the Group Theatre communist "unit" to which he belonged for nineteen months (1934–36), admitting, however, that he did not recall being at a meeting with Gordon. After taking the Fifth Amendment in 1951, Gordon endured eight years on the blacklist before breaking his silence. But in 1948, Michael Gordon was only interested in bringing a drama to the screen. Together, he and Pozner produced an exemplary adaptation of a play, proving as well that art and politics are not inseparable.

Patrolling the Potomac: *Watch on the Rhine*

The success of *Watch on the Rhine*, both the play and the film, is difficult to explain solely in terms of art. The play was well crafted but without the rich characterization of *The Little Foxes;* the film was also tightly constructed but not especially cinematic. Yet the play won the New York Drama Critics' Circle Award. The film won an Academy Award for Paul Lukas as best actor; it was also nominated for best picture but lost to *Casablanca*.

Nevertheless, one must admit that the play, which argued against isolationism when American neutrality was a hotly debated issue, opened on Broadway at exactly the right time—in the spring of 1941, about eight months before Pearl Harbor. Similarly, the film went into nationwide release during the height of World War II—in September 1943. Although the film, like the play, is set in pre–Pearl Harbor America, the plot, which justified fighting against fascism, may have had even greater meaning in 1943 when America was doing precisely that.

Like *The Little Foxes*, *Watch on the Rhine* centered on a family: the Müllers, who were as self-sacrificing as the Hubbards were self-seeking. Kurt Müller is a professional freedom fighter; his American wife, Sara, is the daughter of a distinguished Supreme Court justice. The Müllers have no permanent residence; Kurt, Sara, and their three children go wherever Kurt's work takes him. Currently it has taken him to America, where he is collecting money to aid the victims of fascism. The Müllers stay at the home of Sara's mother, Fanny Farrelly, which is located in a Washington, D.C. suburb. At the moment, Fanny has two other house guests: Count Teck de Brancovis and his wife Marthe. When Teck discovers Kurt's identity and learns that Kurt's briefcase contains $23,000, he attempts to blackmail him, demanding $10,000 in return for concealing his presence from the German embassy. Refusing to pay blackmail with money that had been collected to combat fascism, Kurt kills Teck and returns to Europe to continue his work.

As a play, *Watch on the Rhine* had the kind of drawing-room nobility one might expect of an antiisolationist drama written by an antifascist. It is not a spurious nobility, for Hellman has not written the sort of play that needs patriotic buttressing to shore it up. However, it is a play that one remembers more for its ideas than its theatricality. Frankly, *Watch on the Rhine* lacks the transforming power of theater; the ideas remain inside the dialogue, never turning into images that sear the memory. Unlike Elmer Rice's *Flight to the West* (1941), another antifascist play of the season, *Watch on the Rhine* never leaps out of the proscenium into the hearts of audiences; though it does into their minds. As a thesis play, *Watch on the Rhine* works better as drama than as theater. Because the action never leaves the living room of the Farrelly home, the thesis stays within the setting—a dignified, civilized setting that in turn imparts dignity to the play as well as to the audience.

Because Hellman articulates her ideas so intelligently, *Watch on the Rhine* is still studied as drama, while *Flight to the West*, which is theatrically more effective, would have to be staged to be appreciated. Theater is frailer than drama because dramatic images and stage metaphors are not permanent. Pictures need some means of preservation that suits their evanescent nature. Eloquence requires only print.

Hellman's eloquence inheres within a plot that is constructed around a series of interlocking motifs: the presence of hero and villain under the same roof; their *agon* or confrontation; the object occasioning it (Kurt's briefcase); the resolution (Kurt's murder of Teck); and the romance between the heroine's brother, David Farrelly, and the villain's wife, Marthe de Brancovis. The plot reveals Hellman's knack of matching up characters, balancing opposites, and working out relationships in terms of kinship (Sara and her mother, Sara and her brother); mutual love (Sara and Kurt, Marthe and David); or mutual antagonism (Kurt and Teck). Nowhere is her gift for character alignment better illustrated than in *The Autumn Garden* (1950), which was never filmed and perhaps should not be; *Watch on the Rhine* anticipates *The Autumn Garden* in its marshaling of three groups—the Müllers, the Farrellys, and Teck and Marthe de Brancovis—for the inevitable realignments and shifts of allegiance that come with the unmasking of the villain. Since regrouping often requires elimination, Hellman reduces the three groups to two by killing off Teck and making his death the occasion for Marthe to become a member of another group—the Farrellys. Actually, Marthe's defection from the Axis to the Allies is the result of Hellman's manipulating destiny to effect the kind of pairing off that the plot requires. However, Hellman manages it so well that it seems natural instead of contrived.

For *Watch on the Rhine*, Hellman did a prodigious amount of research, comprising several notebooks of four or five hundred single-spaced typewritten pages of background information. The notebooks even contained three pages of German first and last names. Although these notebooks are unavailable, Margaret Case Harriman, who apparently saw them, believed they could be expanded into a twenty-five-year history of the period.[1]

Hellman's research is apparent in the background she has given her characters. For example, it is not accidental that Teck is Rumanian. Of course, it would have been simpler if she had made the villain a Nazi so that the audience would have no difficulty distinguishing between the "good" German and the "bad" German. But that would have weakened the plot peg (which was not the strongest to begin with). The widow of a Supreme Court justice could entertain a Rumanian count whose allegiance was still undeclared; the time, one must remember, is still pre–Pearl Harbor. But if Fanny Farrelly played hostess to a Nazi, the audience could accept her only as a comic dupe or a stage eccentric, but not as a Washington liberal.

In a drama about fascism, there would be greater contrast if the villain were a member of another fascist country—not an obvious one like Franco's Spain or Mussolini's Italy—but one less familiar, like Rumania. Not only was Rumania fascist; it was also anti-Semitic—two strikes against it in Hellman's eyes. In 1938, King

Carol II gave up any attempt at democracy and established a monarcho-fascist dictatorship. Since Fanny knows her history, she would know about the ultranationalist Iron Guard that championed the peasants, advocating Rumania for Rumanians and calling for the extermination of the Jews. Although Fanny refers to her house guests as "the Balkans" and to being Rumanian as belonging to a profession rather than a nationality, she cannot turn Teck out; one is innocent until proven guilty. But she can express her views with a wit bordering on bluntness. Even in 1944, Hellman was not letting up on Rumania; in *The Searching Wind*, Alex Hazen deplores the way news travels from Rumania, which he dubs "the last stop on the road to misinformation"—a line Hellman retained in her 1946 screenplay. If the news was late, it was because King Carol's power struggle with the Iron Guard impeded the flow of information.

Hellman uses Teck to show that one can turn fascist simply because the winds of change blow in that direction; as usual, she invokes history. Teck left the diplomatic corps in 1931 because of a political miscalculation: he never expected Fritz Thyssen, the Catholic armaments manufacturer and steel tycoon, to support Hitler. Hellman picked the right year for Teck to fall out of favor with the Nazis. In 1931, Thyssen became a member of the National Socialist party, explaining in his fascinating apologia *I Paid Hitler* (1941) that his "sensible and rational" decision was an attempt to save Germany from Communism. Now in disgrace, Teck haunts the German embassy, hoping to exchange some vital piece of information for a visa that would enable him to return to Germany and join the winning side.

Once Teck discovers Kurt's identity, he has his gambit, and Hellman has an opportunity to contrast commitment and opportunism. Kurt, echoing Luther, takes his stand; it is against fascism. But Teck has no stand to take; he simply wants to regain his lost prestige. Otherwise he is uncommitted, morally apathetic. What makes him so frightening is his willingness to acknowledge his bad faith. Hence, the antagonism between Kurt and Teck is not the usual kind that exists between hero and villain; it is a moral confrontation between one who possesses ideals and one who has none.

Just as Teck is not a typical stage villain, so Kurt is not a typical stage hero. Kurt Müller is a historical composite of the resistance hero Rudolf Breda, also known as Otto Katz and André Simone, and Hellman's beloved Julia, an ardent Socialist and antifascist, whom the Nazis killed in 1938 and whose story is told in *Pentimento*. Breda was quite popular in Hollywood in the 1930s, raising funds for the antifascist underground and helping movie liberals like Dorothy Parker, Fredric March, Fritz Lang and others found the Hollywood Anti-Nazi League.[2] Similarly, Kurt's mentor, Max Freidank, who in the play is described as the daredevil of the resistance, seems to have been suggested by Max Hoelz, a kind of Communist Robin Hood.

Hellman envisioned a left-wing hero and vacillated between making him a Communist or a Socialist.[3] Finally, she decided to downplay his politics altogether. When Teck is investigating Kurt, he finds that his dossier at the German embassy reads: "No political connections. No trade union connections." However, Hellman's delineation of Kurt unsettled the Communist press, which criticized her for skirting the issue of his politics, which still seemed decidedly left-wing. The truth is that Hellman was so general in her characterization that Kurt could represent any philosophy, ideology, movement, or religion devoted to the betterment of mankind. That a Communist would see Kurt as a comrade or a fellow traveler is understandable. Kurt is a fund raiser for the victims of fascism; his organization is never specified, although it suggests Willi Münzenberg's Relief Committee for the Victims of Fascism. Kurt served in the International Brigades during the Spanish Civil War. The Brigades were Communist-backed, although not all the Brigaders were Communists. Yet the percentage was high: 60 percent were Communists before volunteering, and 20 percent became Communists afterward.[4]

It might be instructive to compare Kurt with a true stage Communist, Quillery in Robert E. Sherwood's *Idiot's Delight* (1936), who calls everyone "comrade" and extols revolution. Kurt never speaks of the class struggle; he fights against fascism, not for the destruction of the bourgeoisie. He is not a radical, not a Communist, not a Socialist, but a resistance fighter who seems left-wing because the enemy is so totally right-wing. Politically and ideologically, he is an everyman whom any group believing in solidarity, community, and egalitarianism can claim as one of its own.

Theatergoers in the early 1940s would easily recognize Kurt, who, despite his European origins, spoke like a 1930s American liberal. By the mid 1930s, the fascist threat made it possible for liberals, Communists, and Socialists to unite against a common enemy. It was not that the liberals had embraced Marxism or that the Communists had embraced the New Deal; it was simply that a common cause made their differences less apparent: "With the advent of the Popular Front, many liberals found in anti-fascism a cause in which they could be affiliated with the Communists, since the Communists were, in any case, themselves talking very much like New Dealers."[5] Consequently, when the Müllers attack exploitation and oppression or lament a world where hungry men are jailed for stealing bread, they are speaking a liberals' esperanto.

The Müllers retained their universal character in the film version, which did not modify the Popular Front philosophy of the play. Although the movie was not released until the late summer of 1943 (a fact that annoyed Hellman, who had agreed to terminate the play's national tour so the film could go into immediate production), plans for a screen version of *Watch on the Rhine* began shortly after it opened on Broadway. From material in the Warner Brothers archive at the University of Southern California, it is clear that Jacob Wilk, the East Coast story editor at Warner's, initiated negotiations with Hellman and Herman Shumlin, the play's producer-director, for the screen rights.

Warner Brothers was the logical studio for *Watch on the Rhine*. It had made the first major anti-Nazi film, *Confessions of a Nazi Spy* (1939). With America's entry into the war, the Office of War Information recommended that Warner's concentrate on six categories for the duration: enemy, Allies, armed forces, production front, home front, and issues.[6] Wilk realized that *Watch on the Rhine* would make a perfect "issues" movie. Thus he approached Hal B. Wallis, then executive producer at Warner's. Wallis, who had a penchant for movies of political and social consciousness, topical films, and melodramas, agreed that *Watch on the Rhine* would fit into the series of anti-Nazi movies that Warner's was planning—for example, *Dangerously They Live* (1942), *All through the Night*

Hal B. Wallis, the producer of the film versions of *Watch on the Rhine* (1943) and *The Searching Wind* (1946). *(Movie Star News)*

(1942), and *Desperate Journey* (1942). And so, on December 30, 1941, Warner's bought the rights to *Watch on the Rhine* for $150,000.[7]

Since Hellman was still working for Goldwyn, she recommended Hammett for the screenplay, with the understanding that she would come to Hollywood and polish the script before filming began.[8] Thus the credits read: "Screenplay by Dashiell Hammett, Additional Scenes and Dialogue by Lillian Hellman." There is more than a modicum of irony about the credits: in the past, it was Hammett who edited Hellman; in the past, it was Hammett who had the reputation in Hollywood for polishing other writers' scripts.

On 30 January 1942, Warner's signed Hammett to write the screenplay at a salary of $30,000. Wallis expected the script in ten weeks, as stipulated by contract. By mid-February, Hammett had completed a treatment that Wallis liked but that lacked the "big" scene at the end that Wallis wanted. A luncheon meeting with Hellman and Shumlin convinced Wallis that the film should end differently from the play—with the older son carrying on his father's work in the resistance. Thus he told Hammett to think along those lines.

Since Hammett was writing the script at Hardscrabble Farm, Hellman's estate in Pleasantville, New York, Wallis requested it in installments, to be certain his suggestions were heeded. However, Hammett was never a fast writer, and a back injury made him even slower. With prodding from Wallis, Hammett finished the screenplay by mid April. "Wonderful!" Wallis telegraphed, and then proceeded to the all-important matter of casting.

Wallis was able to recruit five members of the original cast: Paul Lukas (Kurt), Lucile Watson (Fanny), George Coulouris (Teck), Eric Roberts (Bodo), and Frank Wilson (Joseph)—as well as the original director, Herman Shumlin. Geraldine Fitzgerald was cast as Marthe, Beulah Bondi as Anise, and Donald Woods as David. Although Bette Davis ended up playing Sara, she was not Shumlin's first choice; he preferred Margaret Sullavan, who was more interested in returning to the stage, and did, in John Van Druten's *The Voice of the Turtle* (1943). Irene Dunne was also considered for the part. Wallis realized that *Watch on the Rhine* needed a female star, even though Sara was not a starring role. Finally, he ap-

proached Bette Davis, who agreed to do it because she believed in
the antifascist theme. Knowing that Kurt was the pivotal role, she
asked for costar billing with Paul Lukas. Although it was a mag-
nanimous gesture, it would not have paid off at the box offiice. To
the public, Bette Davis was the quintessential star. Thus she was
forced to accept star billing to insure the film's success.

With the cast set, *Watch on the Rhine* went before the cameras
on 8 June as scheduled. About a month prior to shooting, Hellman
arrived in Hollywood for a few weeks of script-polishing at $3,000
a week. Except for the dialogue in the scene in which the Müller
children tour Washington, it is difficult to say exactly what Hellman contributed to the screenplay.[9] Whitney Stine claims that the
opening at the Mexican border, the train sequence, scenes at the
German embassy, and a few others are Hellman's.[10] Perhaps, but
without documentation, one can only conjecture. Since Hammett
received screenplay credit, one should assume the script is primarily his; Wallis said as much.[11] In her testimony before the House
Committee on Un-American Activities, Hellman stated that she
"edited" Hammett's screenplay. One may conclude that she did for
his script what he had done for her plays.

Since the screenplay of *Watch on the Rhine* has been published,
one can check it against the film. However, what appears in *Best
Film Plays 1943–44* is not a script with cutting continuity; hence it
will not correspond exactly to what is seen on the screen. For
example, the text of the prologue does not appear in the
screenplay. Still, the discrepancy is not as great as it is, say,
between Ingmar Bergman's published screenplays and his films.

Watch on the Rhine opens with a roll-up prologue extolling the
foresightedness and patriotism of ordinary people, as prologues of
World War II movies often did:

In the first week of April 1940 there were few men in the world
who could have believed that, in less than three months, Den-
mark, Norway, Belgium, Holland and France would fall to the
German invaders. But there were some men, ordinary men, not
prophets, who knew this mighty tragedy was on the way. They
had fought it from the beginning, and they understood it. We are
most deeply in their debt. This is the story of one of these men.[12]

In an early draft of the play, Hellman had the Müllers enter the United States via Mexico. In the play itself, they have been in Mexico, but they have also been in various parts of the United States raising funds for their cause. The film actually opens with the Müllers in Mexico. Apart from being a way of expanding the action beyond the drawing room, the Mexican opening had several other advantages. Historically, Kurt's being in Mexico would make sense since Mexico was pro-Republican during the Spanish Civil War. Thus it does not come as a surprise to learn that Kurt keeps in contact with Mexican antifascists, some of whom undoubtedly contributed to the $23,000 he has collected.

Structurally, the Mexican opening allows two actions to develop simultaneously. While the Müllers are en route to Washington, the Farrelly household is having breakfast—a perfect occasion for exposition. Since the Müllers do not arrive until a good fifteen minutes into the film, the opening sequence unfolds in three segments linked by dissolves so that the action can move back and forth from the Müllers to the Farrellys. It is a long trip the Müllers are making; hence dissolves are more appropriate than cuts, which would denote rapidity. Furthermore, since the opening sequence juxtaposes two actions, the exposition is presented from two points of view, as opposed to the play, in which it was presented from one.

By the time the Müllers have arrived, we know that Kurt fought for the Loyalists in the Spanish Civil War, that Teck consorts with Nazis at the German embassy, and that Marthe and David are in love. But we also know more about the Müllers because we have observed them; they are not the unseen family they were at the beginning of the play. We watch them cautiously going through passport control in Mexico. As they walk together, they seem to share a common identity. They may look like refugees, but there is nothing about the way they move to suggest defeat or demoralization. On the contrary, Kurt is proud of his profession, and his family is proud of him. In the second segment, when the Müllers are on board the train, Bodo boasts to an Italian couple that his father fought in the Spanish Civil War. The Italian man is filled with admiration for Kurt since he too was pro-Republican, although Italy, like Germany, favored the insurgents.

The scene in which the Müllers arrive in Washington is preceded by one that appears to have no relation to them: Teck's attempt to ingratiate himself with influential Nazis at the German embassy. Actually, a subtle cause-effect relationship exists between the two scenes. The second segment ends with Teck's desperately seeking information he can sell in exchange for a visa. The third segment begins with the arrival of the Müllers.

Teck is even more odious than he was in the original because his scheme now affects all the Müllers, not just Kurt. Instead of stressing the romantic or melodramatic aspects of the play, the film focused on the Müllers as a family, something 1943 moviegoers might expect after a succession of movies like *The Pied Piper* (1942), *Mrs. Miniver* (1942), *Happy Land* (1943), and *The Human Comedy* (1943), which dramatized the effect of the war on families. The film also included a concept that was absent in the play: the Müllers' solidarity is not just unity of belief; it is unity of succession. Hammett added a speech in which Kurt tells his older son, Joshua, that he expects him and Bodo to continue his work in the resistance. The Müllers have formed a kind of apostolate in which the sons follow in their father's footsteps.

The film depicts their unity in the very first scene and maintains it to the end; it is even present when Kurt tells his children that he has murdered Teck. However, he does not tell them in the drawing room, as he did on the stage, but in the more intimate setting of the bedroom. Father and children are framed in an unusual four-shot that makes them a real family as opposed to the Farrellys, who remain a stage family—the matriarch and her colorless son. Thus the Müllers evidence greater solidarity than they did on the stage because a film, simply by the way the shots are composed, can depict harmony more graphically.

On the stage, it was all too easy to laugh at the way the Müller children spoke English, as if they were translating directly from the German. But in film, where action is wedded to character, word to image, perception to conception, the characters are what they say. In the play, Bodo, the youngest, just seemed to platitudinize about oppression in splintered English. However, the film makes it clear that Bodo will continue his father's work. The audience therefore believes that Bodo is sincere and not merely precocious; Hammett uses Hellman's dialogue to have him articulate, however pedantically, the Müller credo, thereby providing a dramatic context for Bodo's conviction that one must fight for the good of all men.

In one instance, Hammett reworked a critical line to show that, while the Müllers are peace-loving, they are part of a movement in which violence is inevitable. In the play, Sara noted that many assassination attempts were made on the life of Alfonso XIII of Spain. Bodo's indifference to attempted murder prompts Kurt and Joshua to berate him, for the Müllers deplore violence, even when it is directed against someone like Alfonso XIII, whom they would consider an enemy of freedom. Yet they must—and do—resort to violence.

In the film, they are less rigid in their morality. When Joshua criticizes his younger brother, Bodo does not remain silent as he did in the play. Hammett took an earlier line about Alfonso's "growing fat on the poor" and grafted it on to Bodo's reply which now reads: "Do not give me lessons. It is not right to shoot upon people. . . . Nor is it right to grow fat on the poor people . . ." The change was subtle, but it points up the fact that violence is a response to oppression. The change secularized the Müllers' philosophy by establishing the fact that evil—even murder—cannot always be avoided in the fight for freedom.

When Teck demands $10,000 from Kurt in return for concealing his identity, Kurt has no other choice but to kill him. In the play, the murder was frightening not for the violence (which took place off stage) but for the way the Müllers reacted to it. One had the distinct impression that similar situations had occurred before. Kurt strikes Teck and then orders Joshua in German to drag him outside. Joshua reacts unquestioningly, as if this were a familiar scenario.

In the film, the children are upstairs during the incident. It is Sara who is in the living room when Kurt strikes Teck; it is she who rushes instinctively to the phone and makes a reservation for her husband on the midnight plane to Brownsville. Anticipating what Kurt will do to Teck, she warns her mother to be silent. Kurt also behaves as if he had done this before. As he leads Teck into the garage where he shoots him, Kurt advises him not to speak, knowing from experience that "it is easier without words."

Since Kurt has taught his children that violence is wrong, he

Fascism and Freedom: Teck (George Coulouris) threatens the Müllers (Paul Lukas and Bette Davis) in *Watch on the Rhine*. (*United Artists*)

must explain the murder to them. In both the play and the film, he invoked *Les Miserables,* justifying Teck's murder in the same way Victor Hugo justified Jean Valjean's theft of a loaf of bread, as the act of a starving man—presumably because hunger for freedom is on a par with hunger for food. Admittedly, there is something specious about the logic; Kurt begins by admitting he was wrong and concludes by implying he was right.

However, by Hollywood's standards, Kurt was guilty not of woolly thinking but of violating the Production Code. It seems hard to believe that *Watch on the Rhine* encountered censorship problems, yet it did. About a week before the film went into production, Joe Breen, who at the time was in charge of enforcing the code, reprimanded Jack Warner for allowing a murder to occur without retribution. Breen's philosophy was a variation of the *lex talionis:* if one character takes another's life, the screenwriter must kill him or her off. Breen also objected to the presence of a toilet in a bathroom scene and to some "suggestive" dialogue between David and Marthe that implied they were lovers (which they obviously were). Breen would be satisfied if it were "definitely and unmistakably established with a line of dialogue" that Kurt knows he will be killed if Teck reports his presence to the German embassy; and "if it were clearly and unmistakably established" that, at the end, Kurt is killed by the Nazis. Under these circumstances, "the killing of Teck may be made acceptable on the ground, that in doing this, Kurt is merely preserving his own life, and with the additional indication that, despite all this, Kurt is finally killed in pursuit of his plans."[13]

Circumventing the code was not easy, but it could be done. Astute filmmakers like Ernst Lubitsch, Billy Wilder, and Preston Sturges would resort to various stratagems to keep the Breen office off the primrose path where the film was actually heading—a notable example being Sturges's *The Miracle of Morgan's Creek* (1943), in which unremembered intercourse after a wild night turns out to be post- rather than premarital sex.

Warner and Wallis gave Breen the impression they were following his instructions while, in effect, they were undermining the code. First of all, Kurt never says he will be killed if Teck reports him; in fact, he says the opposite:

TECK: You will not get back if I inform the Embassy you are going. They will see that you are killed before you get there.

KURT: You are wrong. I would get back.

It is Sara who has the line about Kurt's being killed. When David asks increduously, "Is it true that if this swine talks, you and the others . . .?", Sara completes the sentence: "Will be caught and killed."

Kurt's motives for returning to Europe are more complex than self-preservation; there is an enemy to destroy, $23,000 to deliver, and Freidank to rescue. In his screenplay, Hammett stressed the fraternal bond between Freidank and Kurt, changing Sara's matter-of-fact "He loved him" in the play to the stronger "Max and Kurt . . . they loved each other" in the film. It was such a deep love that Max made a medal for Kurt out of his own ring to commemorate Kurt's heroism in Spain.

Furthermore, it is never "clearly and unmistakably established" that Kurt is killed at the end of the film, although one can certainly assume that his family will never see him again. The only scene that might have clarified Kurt's fate was deleted before the film went into release. As has been stated, Wallis wanted a different ending for the film. The play ended with Kurt's departure as Sara, Fanny, and David brace themselves for the difficult days ahead. The movie was to have had two additional scenes. In the first, Kurt is back in Germany with a young man who clearly idolizes him. As Kurt gives the youth instructions for Joshua, the ominous sound of boots is heard on the stairs. In the second, which takes place a few months later in the Farrelly house, Sara realizes that Joshua plans to leave for Europe and join the resistance. In the penultimate scene, Kurt told the young man that one should have children who "will be there to go on." In the final scene, we see the children going on as Joshua reaffirms the principle of succession, instructing his mother to prepare Bodo for the work ahead.

The penultimate scene appears in the published screenplay but not in the film; yet the existence of stills showing Kurt and the young man in a "shabbily furnished room," as Hammett described it, proves that the scene was shot. Ironically, it was the only scene that came close to what Breen wanted. Its deletion, which Wallis sanctioned, did the film no harm since the scene was anticlimactic. Once Kurt leaves, he should not be seen again.

With the deletion of the penultimate scene, it was possible to fade out on Fanny and David, fade in on Joshua's bedroom eight months later, and segue into Hammett's conclusion, in which Sara allows Joshua to go to Europe and agrees to send Bodo when his time has come. This kind of transition, in which a seasonal change—here, the snow falling on the window of Joshua's bedroom—is the link between scenes, was typical of the movies of the 1930s and 1940s. It was also one of the few cinematic touches in

Watch on the Rhine, a film that never quite freed itself from the proscenium.

Perhaps *Watch on the Rhine* was too thesis-bound ever to be cinematic. A director like Wyler might have been able to provide more filmic touches; but one wonders if deep focus and long takes would have solved the problem of a play that was too literary for the screen. One can open a drama up and make the characters more believable, but a drawing-room play never loses its drawing-room sensibility.

The situation was not helped by the fact that Herman Shumlin had never directed a film before. Veteran cameraman Hal Mohr had to mark the camera positions for Shumlin and block the scenes with stand-ins so that, by the time the stars arrived on the set, Shumlin could go through the business of directing.[14] Knowing how important it is in the theater for actors to react to what is happening on stage, Shumlin would shoot entire scenes in which actors without any lines to speak reacted to the dialogue of others. Jack Warner had to remind him not to shoot four full takes of a two-minute scene: "You must remember that our Government has asked us to conserve film." Wallis, who supervised every phase of production, was constantly sending memos to Shumlin asking for retakes, complaining about the slow tempo, recommending more dolly shots, and specifically requesting that Davis be kept in check during her emotional scenes.

Shumlin clearly could not handle Davis. With eyes widened into pools of sorrow and a face reflecting the anguish it was supposed to suppress, Davis delivered her lines as if she were a candidate for early canonization. What she intended as commitment came out as saintliness. There is no denying that *Watch on the Rhine* is a noble work; but it is also possible for a film to be so noble that it ceases to be cinema.

The Moon Is Red: *The North Star*

In *An Unfinished Woman,* Hellman recalls how, early in 1942, she and William Wyler decided to collaborate on a film that would portray the heroic stand the Russians took against Hitler's armies when their homeland was invaded in the summer of 1941. Hellman is vague about the details because, as she notes, she and Wyler did not come to this decision entirely by themselves. There was a man behind the scenes who was interested in their making a pro-Soviet film. He was Harry Hopkins, President Roosevelt's personal adviser and the second most powerful individual in the country. Hopkins, who supported lend-lease to the Soviet Union, envisioned a cinematic tribute to the beleaguered Soviets, who were now our allies. However, a strain of anti-Soviet sentiment still persisted as a result of Stalin's nonaggression pact with Hitler in 1939 and the USSR's invasion of Finland that same year. Even when the Soviet Union was invaded by Germany in June 1941, *Time* magazine called the attack a confrontation between two "prehistorical monsters" of totalitarianism.

Clearly Washington had to find some way to stem the tide of American Russophobia. Since film has always been a powerful instrument of propaganda, Hollywood was prodded into portraying the Soviets as real people instead of the dour lot they appeared to be on the screen. Except perhaps for the atypical *Tovarich* (1937), the Soviets tended to be duplicitous or deluded. In *My Man Godfrey* (1936), a Russian aristocrat sponges off a wealthy family while inveighing against "money, money, the Frankenstein monster." In *Ninotchka* (1939), a female commissar who thought of herself as "a little cog in the great wheel of evolution" orbits out of the party when she discovers haute couture and love, Western style. In

Comrade X (1940), a Soviet streetcar conductor (Hedy Lamarr) forgets Karl Marx when Clark Gable comes into her life.

Hellman's contribution to the new Russia was *The North Star*, one of three pro-Soviet films released in 1943—the others were *Song of Russia* and *Mission to Moscow*—that four years later would be denounced as Red propaganda.

Song of Russia was an innocuous movie about an American symphonic conductor (Robert Taylor) who found love on a concert tour of the Soviet Union. It combined the excesses of the MGM musical and the MGM romance. Ignored in its time, *Song of Russia* became a cause célèbre on 20 October 1947 when writer Ayn Rand appeared before the House Committee on Un-American Activities to testify about alleged Communist infiltration of the motion picture industry. She denounced the film as insidious because it portrayed the Russian peasants as happy when they should have been miserable under communism; and as anti-American because the heroine (Susan Peters) was loath to leave her homeland. She also labeled the film subversive because of a scene in which America faded out and the USSR faded in:

> It starts with an American conductor . . . playing the American national anthem and the national anthem dissolves into a Russian mob, with the sickle and the hammer on a red flag very prominent above their heads. I am sorry, but that made me sick. . . . It suggests literally and technically that it is quite all right for the American national anthem to dissolve into the Soviet.[1]

As a screenwriter herself (*Love Letters*, 1945; *You Came Along*, 1945), Ms. Rand should have known that a dissolve can—and usually does—denote a change of time and place.

Mission to Moscow was based on the 1941 book in which Ambassador Joseph E. Davies recounted his famous trip to the Soviet Union in 1937–38. In Germany, the Davies family witness sights that would make a socialist republic seem like Periclean Athens. A Hitler Youth brigade marches through a Hamburg railroad station where Jews with numbers pinned to their clothes await deportation to concentration camps. Copies of *Mein Kampf* are everywhere, and a uniformed guard informs an elderly couple who missed the train to Leipzig that "the trains of the Third Reich wait for no one."

Once the Davies family arrives in the Soviet Union, the atmosphere changes completely, and so does the lighting—from oppressively dark to cheerfully bright. Even Stalin looks benignly avuncular. Since the film was made to curb anti-Soviet feeling in the United States, Ambassador Davies (Walter Huston) must explain the purge trials, the Russo-German Nonaggression Pact, and the occupation of Finland to the American people. He does so by arguing that the purges were Stalin's attempt to prosecute Trotskyites who were conspiring with Germany to overthrow the Soviet government; that Stalin signed a nonaggresion pact with Hitler to gain time to build up his armies; that the Soviet Union invaded Finland when "Hitler's friend," the Finnish commander-in-chief Marshal Mannerheim, refused its request to occupy strategic positions in Finland despite the Soviet Union's offer of twice as much territory in return! In an attempt to reconcile the red with the red, white, and blue, the film ends with the peoples of the world marching along the road of life as an unseen chorus sings, "You are, yes, you are, you are your brother's keeper, now and fore'er, you are."

The North Star completed the infamous trio; one might call it the best of a not especially distinguished lot. Yet the film has a fascinating history with many questions still unanswered. It was to have been a documentary reuniting Hellman, Wyler, and Toland and shot in the Soviet Union. Wyler and Hellman met with Ambassador Litvinov in Washington; while Litvinov was sympathetic to the project, he felt his country was too preoccupied with the war to give it full support. But the next afternoon, the project was mysteriously approved.

The next hurdle was Sam Goldwyn. In the course of a conference with the producer, the documentary devolved into a semidocumentary, then into a commercial film that would be shot at the Goldwyn studio. Meanwhile, Wyler joined the Army Air Force with the rank of major. The film then acquired a new director, Lewis Milestone. It was at Hellman's request, so Milestone claimed, that he took over for Wyler. In any case, Milestone was a logical choice. He was born in the Ukraine, and the year before had edited *Our*

Russian Front (1942), a documentary assembled from 15,000 feet of Russian newsreel footage. He had directed the antiwar classic *All Quiet on the Western Front* (1930) and was completing *Edge of Darkness* (1943), a powerful account of the Nazi occupation of Norway.

Milestone was not accustomed to dealing with a writer of Hellman's temperament, nor was Hellman used to receiving fifty pages of suggested revisions from a director. Consequently, she bought out the rest of her contract for about $30,000, parting company with Goldwyn after eight years and four films. Goldwyn then brought in Edward Chodorov, who had collaborated on the *Dodsworth* (1936) script, to doctor Hellman's screenplay. His changes were not substantial; the real problem lay in the approach Goldwyn, Milestone, and associate producer William Cameron Menzies took to a screenplay whose chief virtue was simplicity.

The North Star had a simple plot exemplifying one of the oldest techniques in film, the "switchback" or crosscutting of two actions. On 22 June 1941, the day Germany invaded the Soviet Union, five young members of a Ukrainian collective farm called the North Star are hiking to Kiev: Marina (Anne Baxter), Clavdia (Jane Withers) and her younger brother Grisha (Eric Roberts, who also played Bodo in *Watch on the Rhine*), Damian (Farley Granger) and his older brother Kolya (Dana Andrews).[2] The film intercuts their attempt to return home with the events taking place on the farm as the inhabitants prepare for the invaders. The men form a guerilla brigade whose head, Rodion (Dean Jagger), instructs the women to burn their homes before the Germans arrive. When the Germans reach the farm, they find only a few buildings standing, one of which they use as a hospital. The German Dr. Von Harden (Erich von Stroheim) recognizes the Russian Dr. Kurin (Walter Huston), recalling a paper he once delivered at Leipzig. Von Harden respects Kurin, who is appalled by Von Harden's inhumanity. Kurin kills him, but before there can be reprisals, the guerillas return and drive out the Germans. The remaining members of the collective, including the three survivors of the hiking party (Marina, Damian, now blind, and Grisha) pile their possessions on wagons and leave their farm, vowing to "make this the last war."

The film, made from Hellman's screenplay, did not revamp the narrative line; the characters remained the same, and so did the major episodes of the plot. What did change was the concept of the film, which grew from a simple tale of courage into a mammoth production that reproduced the entire collective farm on the studio's ten-acre backlot. William Cameron Menzies, the art director who gave *Gone with the Wind* (1939) its epic style, wanted *The North Star* to have its share of epic moments although it was never intended to have them. Similarly, Milestone used his trademark, the tracking shot, to give the film a sweep that was completely inappropriate. As the children leave for school, the camera accompanies them in a 180-degree circular track that encloses the village within a natural curve. The shot is self-conscious; the context requires simple panning, not majestic tracking. The circular track was part of the circular imagery that dominated the early sequences. To suggest the spirit of communal life, Milestone used circular compositions: peasants dancing in a circle, villagers picnicking in a circle, and a family sitting in a circle during breakfast.

The symbolism would have been easier to take if the film had not been turned into a semimusical. To make the Russians conform to the popular image of men in cossack shirts dancing as they squat with arms folded across the chest, and women in babushkas holding hands as if they were the Graces of the Ukraine, Goldwyn commissioned Aaron Copland to write a score[3] and Ira Gershwin to compose the lyrics. There are four musical numbers in the film, all of them pedestrian. The elders make the girls blush with marriage songs so mundane that one assumes it is embarrassment over the lyrics that brings the crimson to their cheeks. The hikers deliver four lusty choruses about being "the younger generation and the future of the nation." When they display local pride, they do it in the inverted word order of operetta: "Sing me not of other towns / of towns that twinkle and shine." In fact, all the songs sound as if they had been dropped from a second-rate operetta. The nadir is reached in a guerilla chorus with overtones of Sigmund Romberg's *The Desert Song*. As the men ride off, they vow that "the dreams we cherish / will never perish." The same virile refrain is heard again during the end credits, hardly a fitting finale for a war movie that included an assortment of Nazi horrors.

To prove that her screenplay was not a libretto, Hellman had the original script of *The North Star* published in the fall of 1943 to coincide with the release of the film. The edition included a flattering introduction by Louis Kronenberger commending Hellman's eloquence and economy of language; it also contained an author's note in which Hellman explained film terms (cut, dissolve, fade out, etc.) in layman's language.

The screenplay is hardly great literature; it cannot conceal the fact that it originated as propaganda. Since the collective farmers were Communists, Hellman emphasized a feature of Communist life that wartime America could accept: the subordination of self-interest to the common good. When Damian tells Marina that his love for her does not override his love for his country, she understands and smiles proudly at him. The other young Soviets are almost ascetic in their way of life, as if they were postulants in a religious community trying to detach themselves from the world. Clavdia feels the trip to Kiev is enough of a treat and is willing to forego the village supper rather than experience "too many good things at once."

These episodes appear in the actual film; but other details in Hellman's script—details that are ostensibly minor—did not make it to the screen. The scene in which Karp, the pig farmer (Walter Brennan), explains the nature of collectivism is deleted, and the audience is told once—and only once—that the North Star is the name of the collective farm. While the film does not conceal the fact that the setting is a collective farm, it does not stress it, either. Thus in his *New York Times* review, Bosley Crowther commented that the village in the film is "apparently Russian, although the fact is strangely slurred." Hollywood was playing it safe. Kolya the bombardier proudly wears the uniform of the Union of Soviet Socialist Republics, yet as he listens to the radio and breakfasts on pancakes, the scene suggests an American farm rather than a Ukrainian collective.

Hellman planned a folksy opening, with Karp transporting his pigs to market while musing on the inevitability of death. It was not an especially imaginative beginning (pity the actor who must explain destiny to a squealing pig), but the one that Chodorov devised was worse. Karp, now a bearded eccentric, bids good morning to the geese that waddle down the road. As played by Walter Brennan, Karp would be more at home rustling up grub on a cross-country cattle drive than raising pigs for the state. Hellman's village supper was also transformed into an outdoor celebration complete with strolling accordionist and a chorus line led by Clavdia. One assumes it was an excuse for a musical interlude by Copland and Gershwin.

Since the changes in the text were not radical, Hellman could not claim that her screenplay had been substantially rewritten, only that it was given a production that was completely at odds with the theme. Thus Hellman has never disowned *The North Star* and, in fact, told the *New York Times* (19 December 1943) that it was "a valuable and good picture which tells a good deal of the truth about fascism." Naturally, she lamented the way a village festivity was turned into "an extended opera bouffe peopled by musical comedy characters." But her primary objection was the same one that she raised almost a quarter of a century later in regard to another of her screenplays, *The Chase* (1966): the visual style did not fit the script.

In the same interview in which she called *The North Star* "a valuable and good picture," Hellman also called the director "the final arbiter" of a movie and "the last to shape it." Milestone shaped the film along the epic lines that he, Goldwyn, and Menzies had laid down. Yet there were times when Milestone realized Hellman's intentions. There is an exquisite shot, done exactly as Hellman wanted, of Sophia (Ann Harding) braiding the hair of her daughter Marina, who in turn braids the hair of her sister. Milestone was also faithful to Hellman's conception of the scene in which the women set fire to their homes, making it a ritual act that culminates with one of the women walking into the frame, brandishing a kerosene lamp.

Milestone also handled Hellman's two scenes of Nazi brutality with restraint. When Sophia is taken into Nazi headquarters to be tortured, the camera tracks back from the door and moves into the crowd, becoming a spectator. At the very moment it has found its place in the crowd, Sophia's agonized scream is heard. Only later does one see the effects of the torture: a broken arm and leg. Equally restrained in its evocation of horror is the scene in which Von Harden and his assistants take blood from the Russian children to provide plasma for the German soldiers. Hellman's instructions were quite explicit: the doctors were to perform the transfusions with clinical detachment, acting neither inhumanly nor sadistically but with an air of total amorality. Milestone conveyed the dispassionateness of the doctors, but he also portrayed its psychological effect on the children as they sat in the corridor, waiting to be bled. When one of the girls is dragged into the operating room, her hand clutches the wall and then disappears around the corner.

But these are only isolated moments that do not redeem the whole. *The North Star* remains a film of discrete images; some remembered for the wrong reasons (the dancing peasants, the singing guerillas), others too disturbing to forget.

Publisher William Randolph Hearst objected strenuously to *The North Star* and ordered a smear campaign, instructing all of his

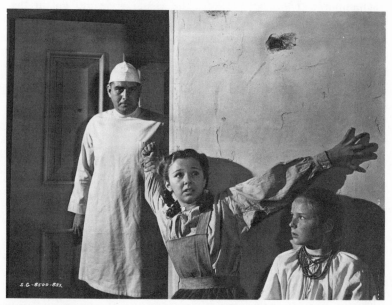

The bleeding of the Russian children in *The North Star* (1943). *(Samuel Goldwyn Productions)*

newspapers to denounce the film as Bolshevik propaganda. However, the directive came a bit late at the New York *Daily Mirror*. Critic Frank Quinn had already written a favorable review that appeared in 1,500,000 copies of the 7 November 1943 Sunday *Mirror*. Then the presses were stopped, and a new review by Jack Lait was inserted in the last 300,000 copies. Thus, depending on which edition one bought, *The North Star* was either "pure bolshevist propaganda" by a screenwriter who was "a partisan pleader for Communist causes" or "a notable tribute to a notable ally."

Generally speaking, the film received good reviews. *Life* not only called it "an eloquent tone poem" but also acclaimed it movie of the year. Actually, *The North Star* turned out to be the movie of three years: 1943, 1947, and 1957.

On 21 October 1947, the day after Ayn Rand denounced the subversive dissolve in *Song of Russia*, actor Adolphe Menjou came before the House Committee on Un-American Activities and denounced *The North Star*, claiming it should never have been made and deploring its inaccuracies: "I also do not think that the picture *North Star* was a true picture, from what I have been able to learn after reading over a hundred and fifty books on the subject."

In 1957, Goldwyn sold *The North Star* to television. He was always ambivalent about it, calling it his greatest film at the time of its premiere and dubbing it "lousy" a year later. National Telefilm Associates (NTA) reedited *The North Star*, changing its title to *Armored Attack* and not *Armored Train* as Hellman states in *An Unfinished Woman*. *Armored Attack* appeared on television a year after the Hungarian uprising of 1956 when many who had earlier been pro-Soviet were condemning Soviet aggression. The screen credits identify it as "An Adaptation of the Motion Picture *The North Star*"; Hellman is acknowledged as author of the "Original Screenplay and Story."

The reedited version is a perfect illustration of how the original intention of a film can be modified or reversed. As a result of voice-over commentary, scenes that once engendered sympathy for the Russians now have the opposite effect. In *The North Star*, the credits appeared against a background of pastoral tranquillity; in *Armored Attack*, they coincide with one of the most ominous shots in the film: Von Harden's armored car moving against a sky of threatening gray.

No sooner does Karp appear on the screen than a sober voice is heard off-camera, sounding as if it were emanating from a tabernacle: "This is the story of a people betrayed, who defended their homes and children only to see them destroyed by the arms of a godless invader. It is the story of how they met the attack and how they fought back." The meaning is garbled. Who was betrayed and to whom? If one unscrambles the thinking, the voice is really saying that the Russians were betrayed by their own people.

Immediately after Kolya and his family hear a radio report of children bled to death and of German troops massing on the Polish border, the omniscient voice continues: "Because their leaders told them there is no danger, the reports from the West have little meaning." Again the expression is confused. First, we are never told who these leaders are. Are they the chairmen of the collective farms or Stalin himself? In either case, there was no betrayal. Stalin mistakenly believed that Germany would not attack the Soviet Union although Roosevelt and Churchill warned him an invasion was imminent. Equally misleading was the implication that the radio report of Nazi atrocities and troop maneuvers was coming from the West (presumably via Voice of America) when it could only be originating from Moscow.

As the film continues, the commentary becomes more solemn. After the men take the guerilla oath, the voice laments that their village will be "crushed between (sic) the steel treads of the attacking tanks." In the same breath, the voice speaks of "the consequences of betrayal," again creating a false distinction between a country invaded and a country betrayed.

The voice is unusually strong at the end of Armored Attack. In The North Star, Marina, vowing "to make a free world for all men," delivered the closing lines: "The earth belongs to the people. If we fight for it. And we will fight for it." Since NTA deleted every "comrade" from the film, one would hardly expect Marina's peroration to be retained, evoking as it does a revolutionary's clenched fist. Instead, the voice tautologically reminds us that "Marina spoke for all the people everywhere." It goes on to remind us that times have changed:

Today, as in all dictatorships, the lie, the double cross and the sell-out build the Communist dream of empire. The Nazi war machine has been replaced by the armor of the Soviets. The gallant struggle of the Hungarian freedom fighters stands as a shining symbol of man's love of freedom. Perhaps some day there will be an end to bloodshed. But until that day every person and every nation must be aware of the menace of Communism.

Apart from its self-righteousness, the epilogue is pure Procrustean bed manipulation in which the facts are stretched into shapelessness to fit a thesis. There is also a total absence of logic as sentences are strung together without ever combining to form a central thought. An allusion to the Nazis is followed by a tribute to the Hungarians, complete with a newsreel shot of a Soviet tank patrolling a street in Budapest.

The North Star, which originated as pro-Soviet propaganda in 1943, became anti-Soviet propaganda fourteen years later by the addition of a voice that delivered a running commentary on the action and by the incorporation of newsreel footage that equated the Soviet Union's 1956 suppression of the Hungarian uprising with Germany's 1941 invasion of the Soviet Union. Eisenstein was not exaggerating when he claimed that the possibilities of film are unlimited.

What Price Appeasement: *The Searching Wind*

Hellman's fifth play, *The Searching Wind* (1944), completed the World War II trio she began with *Watch on the Rhine* and followed with the screenplay of *The North Star*. Although these works were based on contemporary history and were extensively researched, Hellman has never attempted a historical drama on the order of Robert Bolt's *A Man for All Seasons* (1960) or John Osborne's *Luther* (1961). The closest she came to historical drama were two plays that she adapted for Broadway: *Montserrat* (1949), based on Emmanuel Roblès's play of the same name, which was set in Venezuela in 1812, when Simon Bolivar was attempting to free the country from Spanish rule; and *The Lark* (1955), her reworking of Jean Anouilh's play about Joan of Arc, *L'Alouette*.

However, Hellman's method is not so different from a historical playwright's. A historical playwright dramatizes the interrelationship between actual personages and their times, showing the impact of the individual on the age and vice versa. Hellman places fictional characters, sufficiently representative of their times, in a historical setting. In *The Searching Wind*, her most ambitious play although not one of which she is especially fond, Hellman illustrated the connection between appeasement on the personal and international levels; she made her protagonist an ambassador whose inability to choose between his wife and his mistress was symptomatic of a world that could not choose between enslavement and freedom.

Alex Hazen chose a career that would prevent his ever having to take a stand; as an ambassador, he could conciliate and appease, but not act independently. His wife, Emily, is the daughter of the liberal newspaper publisher, Moses Taney. However, Emily has acquired none of her father's convictions; she actually revels in the role of the nonpartisan hostess who must be gracious to everyone, including the Nazis seated on either side of her at dinners. Cassie Bowman, a college teacher and Alex's mistress, alone has moral convictions; she tries to be Alex's conscience, but the role she has assumed—the backstreet woman who summers in Europe so she can be near her lover—allows her only to plead with Alex to "do something" and express disappointment when he does not. Yet even Cassie is not faultless; when she indicts her generation as "frivolous," she is including herself.

Whatever misgivings Hellman may have had about the play (she thought it was too political to be good theater), structurally it is her most intricate. It is told in flashbacks which, while they are sequential (1922, 1923, 1938), exist as scenes within acts rather than as separate acts. Consequently, there is an interaction between present and past that would not have been possible if each flashback had been given an act to itself. *The Searching Wind* is written in two acts of three scenes each. The main action and the play itself begins with Cassie's arrival at the Hazens' Washington, D.C. home on a spring evening in 1944. Scene 2 is a flashback to 1922, while scene 3 returns the action to the Hazens' drawing room. The second act is almost the reverse, beginning in 1923 (scene 1), proceeding to 1938 (scene 2), and concluding with 1944 (scene 3). Hellman will use a similar approach in "Julia," the most famous sketch in *Pentimento*, in which a particular year, 1937, becomes a conduit to the tunneled past through whose passages the author tries to find her way.

The film version of *The Searching Wind* appeared two years after the play. Hal B. Wallis had left Warner's as chief of production in 1943 and the following year formed his own production company with headquarters at Paramount, the studio through which his films would now be released. Wallis had produced many films of social and political consciousness at Warner's: for example, *I Am a Fugitive from a Chain Gang* (1932), *The Story of Louis Pasteur* (1935), *Marked Woman* (1937), and *They Made Me a Criminal* (1939). Since *Watch on the Rhine*, one of the last pictures he produced at Warner's, was such a popular success, he was interested in another

Hellman play. As an independent producer, Wallis was able to hire Hellman to write her own script. Clearly *The Searching Wind* was not a typical Paramount picture of the postwar era; more representative of the studio were *Blue Skies* (1946), with Bing Crosby, and *Monsieur Beaucaire* (1946), with Bob Hope. Even the leads were not Paramount regulars: Robert Young (Alex) and Sylvia Sidney (Cassie). Ann Richards (Emily) had been at Paramount for only about a year.

Wallis apparently wanted something similar to *Watch on the Rhine:* a civilized film that argued for commitment in the language of the drawing room. As *The Searching Wind*'s director he picked William Dieterle, with whom he had worked at Warner's on such films as *The Story of Louis Pasteur, The Life of Emile Zola* (1937), and *Juarez* (1939). The German-born Dieterle was able to give the European sequences an air of authenticity; he was also able to counterbalance the romantic and historical aspects of the plot. The year before he did *The Searching Wind*, Dieterle directed Wallis's second independent production for Paramount, *Love Letters* (1945), in which he had to integrate romance and melodrama, never allowing the sensational part of the plot (murder followed by amnesia) to obscure the Cyrano de Bergerac story of a man who wrote a friend's love letters.

The credits of *The Searching Wind* appear against a background of trees swaying in the wind to the music of Victor Young's score, which is tender without being lush. The title is no more explained in the film than it was in the play; it was a phrase Hellman heard one of her maids use to describe a wind that penetrated to the bone. Within the context of the plot, the "searching wind" is history blowing through the hollow men, reminding them of their emptiness; it is the chill of guilt that leads to an admission of failure and inadequacy. Yet the film is also a love story; the wind that searches the conscience also searches the heart and finds it equally wanting. Dieterle did not lose sight of the fact that *The Searching Wind* was a romantic drama played against a historical background in which political compromises were not qualitatively different from personal ones.

Like *Dead End, The Little Foxes*, and *Watch on the Rhine, The Searching Wind* also opens with a printed prologue. However, the prologue is really an epigraph, an excerpt from Roosevelt's report from the 1945 Yalta Conference, in which he accused the world leaders of failing the men who in 1914–18 fought the war to end war: "We failed them then. We cannot fail them again, and expect the world to survive, again."

It was a fitting epigraph, for it was the failure of the post–Versailles world that formed the basis of the film. Roosevelt's accusation reverberates throughout the final scene when the Hazens' son, Sam, who must lose a leg because of a war injury, rebukes his parents for their lack of commitment. Sam accepts his sacrifice but insists that his elders acknowledge what their neutrality has cost the young. Sam is the voice of his parents' conscience—the wind that chills them into self-awareness.

Unlike the play, in which the amputation of Sam's leg was reserved until the end, the film emphasized it from the outset because Hellman wanted to establish the fact that Sam's suffering was mental as well as physical. She therefore revised the opening so that the film would not begin as the play did—with an exchange between Sam and his grandfather, Moses Taney—but with Alex and Moses trading insults. As Alex rearranges his files, Moses wonders why his son-in-law wants to preserve his mistakes: "I can remember mine. You've made so many, I suppose it is more difficult for you to remember them all." But Hellman knows when to terminate the quips; a scream brings them to an end. Sam is waking from a nightmare; he is haunted by memories of the war that claimed his best friend and that will claim his leg the next morning.

Although, as we shall see, Hellman made other changes for the film version (for example, the addition of a new flashback and a few minor characters), she did not alter the play substantially. She kept the framing device of the dinner party that brought Alex, Emily, and Cassie together. The play's structure was sufficiently cinematic that it did not have to be disturbed. The chief difference between the play and the movie is that, in the latter, there is one uninterrupted flashback. Of course, Hellman could have fashioned the screenplay so the action would return periodically to the dinner table. However, she and Dieterle found a way of preserving the connection between the past and the present: the flashback begins with Cassie and is presumably narrated by her, but is witnessed by Sam. Thus it is Sam who is the link between the errors of the past and their atonement in the present, for it is he who sees the world his parents' generation created—a generation whose like Cassie hopes will never exist again.

Hellman provided the motivation for the flashback, Dieterle the visual bridge. When news of Mussolini's execution comes over the radio, Alex toasts "the end of one more villain"; but Moses recalls a time when Alex did not consider Mussolini a villain—in 1922, to be precise. Now the time of the main action is clearly specified; unlike the general "Spring 1944" of the play, the film begins on 28 April 1945. Thus the flashback to Rome, 1922 is better motivated than it was in the play. It also draws the trio into a circle of irony: Cassie, Alex, and Emily, who were in Rome on the evening of 28 October 1922 when Mussolini marched on the city, are reunited on the evening of his death.

However, someone else is drawn into this shared memory— Sam, who becomes the visual and moral center of the flashback. We hear the off-camera voices of Cassie and Emily recalling the evening they were at the salon of Mrs. Hayworth, a wealthy American living in Rome. Yet it is Sam's face we see on the screen as the women speak. The camera tracks up to him and, when he is framed in close-up, a wavy wipe moves across the screen, giving the effect of a billowing curtain drawn over Sam's face. Then the shot dissolves to one of a real curtain, which Emily draws aside to reveal Mrs. Hayworth's salon in which a concert is about to take place. Sam too has entered the past with the others. For the past is the present's legacy, an idea Hellman reiterates in her plays and particularly in her third memoir, *Scoundrel Time* (1976), in which she argued that the silence during the McCarthy era led to Vietnam and Watergate. In *The Searching Wind*, she made World War II the culmination of a policy of appeasement the world embarked upon after Versailles—a policy Sam's father helped carry out.

The 1922 flashback is more powerful in the film than it was in the play because of the salon sequence that Hellman created especially for the screen version. Her intention was to dramatize the dangerous naiveté of Americans like Mrs. Hayworth, who welcomes Fascists to her home and extols the "glory that has returned to Rome with Mussolini," and Emily, who is being courted by a Fascist eager to explain why Mussolini is so necessary to his country. Hellman had another reason for beginning the 1922 segment with the salon episode: it led directly to another scene that she transferred from the play—the scene in which an Italian waiter tells Moses how the United States failed Italy in 1919, the year Mussolini formed the first cell of his fascist party. Thus 1922 is the result of 1919, just as each event in the flashback is a link in a concatenation of events and forces slowly encircling Europe.

In 1922, however, Alex still had the rudiments of a conscience. When Mrs. Hayworth asks the orchestra to play "Giovinezza," the Fascist anthem, he and Cassie—now a journalist instead of a teacher—walk out of the salon, although one wonders if he would have had the courage to leave had he been alone. Alex's courage soon dissipates. As long as he is with Cassie, who believes it is better to do something than to do nothing, he has some principles; once he falls under Emily's spell, he loses the few he had. When he fails Cassie by not reporting the truth about Mussolini, she refuses to marry him and requests a transfer to Paris. Alex insists he cannot take sides, to which Cassie replies in language that is immediately identifiable as Hellman's: "Whenever people talk about not taking sides, they've already taken one." With Cassie gone, Emily can complete his apolitical education.

The Rome, 1922 segment ends with Alex and Emily on the verge of marriage, not because they really love each other but because Cassie, their conscience, is no longer there to prod them. Since the flashback is continuous, the years that are not dramatized are depicted in montage, with newspaper headlines superimposed on each other to portray the passage of time. This device is known as American montage to distinguish it from montage in the European sense of cutting—the step-by-step assembling of the shots that make up the film. American montage is a familiar way of collapsing time. When it is successful, as it is here, it achieves the effect of an uninterrupted flow of time, as the following outline shows:

Segment 1   Rome, 1922
                Montage (1922–28): Cassie's columns in *Washington Bulletin* juxtaposed with international headlines culminating in NEW NATIONAL SOCIAL-

IST PARTY IN GERMANY BLAMED FOR UNSETTLED CONDITIONS

Segment 2   Berlin, 1928
Montage (1928–36): Headlines superimposed on shots of Alex, last headline reading CIVIL WAR IN SPAIN: PROOF OFFERED THAT ITALY AND GERMANY AIDING FRANCO WITH MEN, PLANES, AND GUNS

Segment 3   Madrid, 1936
Montage (1936–38): Headlines again superimposed on shots of Alex, giving way to ticker tape crossing screen: PROCEED VIENNA . . . REPORT ON ANSCHLUSS

Segment 4   Paris, 1938

The montage in *The Searching Wind* is ingeniously done; it not only crystallizes the events leading to World War II but also gives them a configuration. Such historical montage is rare in Paramount films of the period; one associates it with Warner Brothers, where Don Siegel, later to become a well-known director, set up a montage department and bridged the gaps in such films as *Casablanca* (1942) and *Action in the North Atlantic* (1943). Wallis, who produced several of the films, including *Casablanca,* for which Siegel did the montages, may well have been applying a Warner Brothers touch to a Paramount movie.

The first montage sequence ends as the 1928 segment begins with Cassie in Berlin covering a Nazi rally; a figure, silhouetted against a flag, shrieks his message to roaring approbation. She sits stone-faced at the rally; next to her is a woman with a child in a brown shirt, a future Hitler Youth. Cassie and the child represent a sad juxtaposition of the free and the enslaved, of experience that still has its youthful zeal and innocence that has been lost before its time. Cassie, who would not give the fascist salute in Rome, remains seated during the singing of the German anthem.

Cassie's next encounter with Alex in the play occurred in 1923; in the film, Hellman defers it to 1928, when National Socialism was a greater threat. Thus Cassie's original line, "Hard to believe that we would live to see a pogrom in the year 1923," becomes "It's hard to believe that we would live to see anything like this in the year 1928"—"this" being an attack on a Jew by Nazi hoodlums shouting racial obscenities. A similar incident is mentioned in the play, but it is more intense in the film because of the setting in which it occurs—a fashionable restaurant in which Alex is having lunch. Alex has not changed in the past six years; he predicts that National Socialism will disappear with better times. He is the type who could be expected to view the conflict between the Loyalists and the Nationalists in Spain as just a civil war.

To contemporary historians, the Spanish Civil War was the dress rehearsal for World War II. It was a war that made lasting friendships or mortal enmities depending on which side one favored: the Loyalists, who supported the Republic, or the Nationalists, who sought to restore the power of the church, the army, and the aristocracy. Hellman favored the Loyalists, although her position would cost her friends—Mary McCarthy, for one, who would not support the Loyalists because they were receiving aid from the USSR. However, Hellman's stand was hardly unique; other pro-Loyalist writers included Ernest Hemingway, W. H. Auden, André Malraux, George Orwell, C. Day Lewis, Dorothy Parker, and Rex Warner.

When Hellman visited Spain in 1937, she was convinced she had made the right choice. One does not know if she was aware that both sides were guilty of atrocities; to her, the Spanish Civil War was a battle between the forces of freedom and fascism. It was for this reason that she agreed to write the narration for the antifascist film documentary, *The Spanish Earth* (1937), that Joris Ivens shot behind the Loyalist lines. However, a bout with pneumonia in Paris prevented her from joining Ivens in Spain, and Hemingway, who was already in Spain, did the narration. However, Hellman was a member of Contemporary Historians, the group that produced the documentary and that also included Herman Shumlin, Archibald MacLeish, and Hemingway.

It was natural, then, for Hellman to include the Spanish Civil War in the film of *The Searching Wind*, for it was the link between the rise of National Socialism and the Munich Agreement, which saw its triumph in 1938. She could not have included it in the original; a war episode would have been out of place in a drama that did not depict war but only its prelude. It would also have been

Cassie (Sylvia Sidney) and Alex (Robert Young) embroiled in a love affair while Spain is embroiled in civil war in *The Searching Wind*. (MCA Publishing)

difficult to explain Cassie's presence in Madrid during the conflict because she was originally a teacher. Since she is now a journalist, her presence in Madrid in 1936 is completely appropriate.

The transition from Berlin, 1928 to Madrid, 1936 is a torchlit Nazi rally with *flambeaux* outlined against the sky—a vivid suggestion of the coming holocaust. The montage that follows is equally ominous; juxtaposed against the news of the day are shots of Alex advancing in his diplomatic career as the world advances toward war. As the last headline fills the screen announcing Italian and German aid to the Nationalists, an air raid sends people streaming into a cellar café in Madrid.

Cassie is there with some other reporters, one of whom complains about salary and another of whom dismisses the bombings as scare tactics. Alex enters the café and, in a high angle shot, he sees Cassie, her back to the camera. As she turns around, there is an explosion. Amid rubble and death, Alex confesses his love for

Cassie, who is torn between her affection for him and her contempt for his political stance. In language considerably stronger than any she had used in the play, Cassie berates Alex for not reporting that German planes are bombing Madrid. "You have nothing to do with death because you have nothing to do with people," she cries. "You're a diplomat." It is Hellman speaking through Cassie; Hellman, "afraid of being afraid," voicing her fears through a character who will not let her fear stand in the way of action.

The figure of Alex also dominates the final montage, which covers the years 1936–38. Ticker tape moving across the screen bears instructions for Alex to fly to Vienna and report on the *Anschluss*, the union of Austria and Germany that was effected in March 1938 and amounted to Hitler's takeover of Austria. Finally, we are in Paris for the last segment of the flashback. Emily has grown more apolitical and indiscreet, dining with Nazis and swallowing the myth that Hitler would be appeased with the annexation of the Czech Sudetenland.

On the evening Alex is to write his report on the rape of Czechoslovakia, he is visited by Count Von Stammer, who typifies the effect of totalitarianism on the spirit. He is an effete, doddering old man—an androgynous amalgam of crone and wizard. Proudly apathetic and interested only in buying a leather briefcase and a house in Switzerland, he wants Alex's assurance that he will not condemn Hitler's annexation of the Sudetenland. Alex agonizes over his report, and it is only when Emily begs him to be noncommittal so that their son, Sam, will not have to go to war that Alex concedes. It is the only time in the film that one is moved by Alex's dilemma, even though his position saved neither Sam nor Sam's generation from war. At first, Alex is in a denunciatory mood, protesting "the easy giving over of Czechoslovakia to the arrogant Germans." But he gradually softens the tone, deleting controversial language and anti-Nazi sentiments until the report is diplomatic doublespeak.

The flashback comes to a poignant end at the airport, where the occupation of the Sudetenland is announced over a loudspeaker. An elderly man walks out of the airport, holding a handkerchief to his eyes. Emily, waiting in a car, pulls the shade down so Cassie will not see her. Cassie's shadow against the car dissolves to the Hazens' dining room. The flashback ends as it began, with a close-up of Sam's face. He has had a crash course in the history of the period between the wars and is critical of the role his parents played during it.

After Cassie leaves, Sam delivers pretty much the same speech he gave in the play. For the film, Hellman modified the tone so that at least Sam admits that he loves his parents. However, he will also be losing a leg in the morning; still, if his leg will change people's thinking, "everybody's welcome to it." "America the Beautiful" on the soundtrack is strangely fitting at this point, although ordinarily it is a patriotic cliché.

In the play, Hellman had Sam ask: "How do you say you love your country?" Since she wanted the film to end on a note of hope, she added some new dialogue. Originally, Sam's question about love of country was a rhetorical one. In the film, Emily answers it: "I don't know. We're frightened of saying things like that because we might sound like the fakers who do say them." If his mother can't say them, Sam can; he is not a faker. After professing his love for America, he repeats a line from the play: "And I don't want any more fancy fooling around with it." Nor, one assumes, does Lillian Hellman.

The film's ending is really one of guarded optimism. Alex and Emily will not divorce, for, as Cassie has noted, they are too much alike. Whether they will change is problematical, although they have been chastened by the evening. Cassie found them wanting; Sam found them irresponsible. Although Cassie included herself in the generation she deplored, she has at least tried to live up to her principles. As the film opens, she is shown getting into trouble with her editor for mentioning that his son-in-law was decorated by Hitler in 1938. Like Hellman, Cassie would not cut her conscience to fit the current fashions.

In *The Searching Wind*, Hellman gave moviegoers a clear and vivid dramatization of the major events and movements that led to World War II. In most World War II movies made in the 1940s, history was the backdrop for the plot; in *The Searching Wind*, it was embedded in the action like the tiles in a mosaic.

The Steamy South: *Toys in the Attic* and *The Chase*

After *The Searching Wind*, Hellman would not write another screenplay for twenty years. However, this need not have been the case. In *Scoundrel Time*, Hellman recalls how, in 1947, Harry ("White Fang") Cohn, head of Columbia Pictures, offered her a million-dollar, eight-year contract allowing her to write and pro-duce, "without interference," four films of her choice with the right of final cut. All she had to do was sign an affidavit stating that she would not consort with radicals or subversives and, most impor-tant, that she was not a Communist. Arguing that a loyalty clause was a violation of one's constitutional rights, Hellman refused to sign it. Shortly afterwards, she learned from William Wyler, who wanted her to write the screenplay for his film version of Dreiser's *Sister Carrie*, that she had been blacklisted.

Without a loyalty oath, Hellman would be unemployable in Hollywood. The man with whom she lived, Dashiell Hammett, was a Marxist and, as Hellman conjectures, probably a Communist. The sides she took and the causes she supported in the 1930s—the Loyalists in the Spanish Civil War, the Hollywood Anti-Nazi League which the House Committee on Un-American Activities considered a Communist front—made her suspect at a time when the movie industry itself was being investigated for Communist subversion.

In addition to being a blacklisted screenwriter, she also seemed to be turning into an unsuccessful playwright. *Montserrat* and *The Autumn Garden*, which scholars now regard as her best play, were failures. In fact, between 1949 and 1960, Hellman had only one Broadway hit, and it was not even an original work; it was *The*

Lark, her adaptation of Anouilh's *L'Alouette*. Then, on 25 February 1960, her fortunes revived when *Toys in the Attic* opened in New York for a run of 464 performances.

In *Toys in the Attic*, Hellman returned to a theme that had personal as well as dramatic significance: money, its fascination and abuse. The main character is the raffish Julian Berniers, who returns to his New Orleans home with his childlike bride, Lily, and an embarrassment of gifts for his two unmarried sisters, Anna and Carrie. Initially, the sisters are overwhelmed by the presents, which include fur-trimmed coats, diamond-initialed handbags, and boat tickets to Europe. Soon, however, Carrie starts to resent the chaos Julian's sudden wealth has brought into her life, particularly the way it has upset her routine and given the house the air of a bordello. One senses it will be only a matter of time before the fool and his money are parted, but one does not realize how tragic that parting will be.

Eventually Carrie learns the money came from some real estate that Julian sold to a shady lawyer, Cyrus Warkins, knowing in advance that Warkins needed the property for a deal of his own. The source of Julian's information was Charlotte Warkins, the lawyer's wife and Julian's former mistress. Lily, believing her husband will leave her for Charlotte, is willing to sacrifice their wealth if this will enable her to keep him. She phones Warkins, begging him to ask Charlotte to give up Julian just for a year. Carrie stands by during this incredible conversation and even makes it possible for Warkins to take revenge on Julian and Charlotte by disclosing their meeting place to Lily. Warkins dispatches his thugs, who rob Julian of the money and slash Charlotte's face so she will be permanently disfigured.

If the mood of *Toys in the Attic* struck some theatergoers as uncommonly dark, it may, in part, have been because, while she was writing it, Hellman had before her the spectacle of Hammett's progressively deteriorating health. Within a year of the Broadway opening, Dashiell Hammett would be dead; but the royalties Hellman received during that time made it possible for her to give him the comforts of the dying. The sight of Hammett wasting away from inoperable lung cancer may also have contributed to the way Hellman delineated the main characters, who appear as transmogrified versions of herself, her father, and her aunts. Lily is a self-caricature; Julian was suggested by the playwright's father, Max Hellman; Carrie and Anna are exaggerated portraits of her maiden aunts, Jenny and Hannah. Ironically, Hellman preferred her father's family to her mother's. In *An Unfinished Woman,* she writes: "It was not unnatural that my first love went to my father's family. He and his two sisters were free, generous, funny," although one would never know it from the play.

Therefore, it is best to take *Toys in the Attic* as Doris Falk does—as a work that "plays imaginatively with what *might* have happened" to Hannah, Jenny, and Max Hellman if they had not been free, generous, and funny but rather unpredictable, neurotic, and destructive.[11] The play also invites us to consider what might have become of Lillian Hellman if she had continued to be as intoxicated with truth as she was as a child. She could easily have become like Lily, whose obsession with truth caused the loss of a fortune and a woman's disfigurement. As a child, Hellman went through what she called in *Pentimento* a "religious truth kick," swearing on the steps of a cathedral that she would never lie. Often this devotion to the cause of truth led the young Hellman to meddle in the affairs of others and, on one occasion, to jeopardize another's future—her cousin Bethe's. In "Bethe," the opening sketch of *Pentimento,* Hellman describes the way she pursued her cousin and insisted on seeing her even though Bethe was living with a gangster. In *Toys in the Attic,* Hellman relegated truth to the level of destructive candor, turning it into a weapon the characters use against each other. As Lily's mother, Albertine, notes at the end of the play, one can "kill . . . with the truth."

Toys in the Attic might have been a major film if the screenwriter, James Poe, had been able to distill some of the play's subtlety into his script. Poe, who specialized in adapting the works of southern writers, had written the screenplays for Tennessee Williams's *Cat on a Hot Tin Roof* (1958) and *Summer and Smoke* (1961), and Faulkner's *Sanctuary* (1961). Unfortunately, Poe believed that audiences would accept a higher degree of exaggeration in a movie with a southern setting than they would in a film set in some other part of the country. Still, it is one thing to make characters "outrageous," as Poe claims one can if they are Southerners; it is another to make them ludicrous. Poe reduced the South to the two s's: sweltering and sexy. Even the opening has a neon look. In the credits sequence, Lily (Yvette Mimieux) leaves a hotel and walks down a New Orleans street as the names of the cast appear in marquee lettering on the facades of buildings and along the pavement. Later, one sees Julian and Lily in a cheap hotel; it is movie sex, "Southron style": rumpled sheets, sleeveless undershirts, and clinging slips. Heat is everywhere, including the Berniers home, where the metaphors are more genteel. With a ladylike twist of her fingers, Carrie (Geraldine Page) unbuttons the top of her dress and stands in front of a fan.

It has never been Hellman's practice to explain the meaning of a title within the play itself, although the title symbolism of *Toys in the Attic* is easily inferred: clinging to the past results in behavior that is dangerously immature, for it reduces adults to children clutching toys that should have been discarded at the end of childhood and speaking with a searing openness that only the naive would call truth. Poe chose to dramatize the title symbolism. Julian (Dean Martin) arrives at the house when Carrie and Anna (Wendy Hiller) are in the attic. Anna wistfully runs her hand across an old hobby horse, and Carrie hugs one of Julian's trophies as if it were Julian himself. "Is that my Carrie hiding in the attic?" Julian calls as he enters. The line is so self-consciously symbolic that it forces the audience to take the scene in the attic as a metaphor of regression instead of allowing the audience to come to that conclusion on its own.

Except for an added and qualified happy ending, Poe followed the basic outline of Hellman's plot. However, he was unable to duplicate her infallible sense of rhythm. Hellman is uncommonly good at building an action to an emotional climax. Tensions peak at the right moment; erratic outbursts that would hinder the drama's spiraling motion are avoided. But in the film, the action does not spiral; it zig zags. Carrie starts railing at Julian much too early—on the first evening, in fact. Her jealousy and anger then become wearisome because they have been displayed too soon and too quickly.

Hellman also knew that, with certain characters, no more should be revealed than necessary, a rule Poe did not follow in regard to

Lily's mother, Albertine. Hellman's Albertine radiated the aloofness of wealth and spoke with an epigrammatic hauteur as if all life were a salon over which she presided. Hellman kept an air of mystery about her, giving her dialogue that enabled her to speak with the authority of an oracle. When Lily expresses her hatred of money, Albertine replies: "Then be very careful. Same thing as loving it." Albertine can also mingle wit and insult: "There are many ways of loving. I'm sure yours must be among them."

Poe's Albertine (Gene Tierney), on the other hand, neither exudes mystery nor turns a memorable phrase. She is a wealthy eccentric who talks to Julian as if he were a crony. In the play, Albertine found him amusing and somewhat touching, the way a queen might regard a court jester whose antics were more pathetic than entertaining.

Poe's screenplay was not the kind to challenge a director's visual sense, and George Roy Hill gave it the kind of perfunctory direction it merited. However, in the scene in which Warkins's thugs attack Julian and Charlotte, Hill went beyond the perfunctory. Julian and Charlotte are walking along the pier when a baggage trolley appears behind them, forcing them into a corner. Hill uses a high shot to express their helplessness; then he switches to a medium shot, and finally to a close medium shot—mercifully, not an extreme close-up—of Charlotte's face being slashed by a razor.

Poe modified the ending, making Carrie the loser and giving her a semimad scene that Geraldine Page played with a shrillness that was more ludicrous than lunatic. In the play, Lily, at her mother's insistence, never told Julian she was responsible for Charlotte's disfigurement. In the film, she admits her guilt and receives the conventional slap across the face from Julian—much to Carrie's delight. However, when Julian realizes his sister is exulting in his misfortune, he rushes out of the house, presumably to return to Lily. A repentant wife is preferable to an unregenerate sister. Carrie raves for a moment; then her raving changes to delirium as she imagines Julian coming back and taking her in his arms. But the strain of fantasy is too much, and Carrie collapses on the stairs—the camera peering down on her in a high shot as if she too had become a toy for the attic.

The film was generally panned, and some of the reviews even

The battered Julian Berniers (Dean Martin) embracing his sister Anna (Wendy Hiller) and leaving Carrie (Geraldine Page) with one less "toy in the attic." *(United Artists)*

criticized Hellman although she had nothing to do with the movie version. In his *New Republic* review (17 August 1963), Stanley Kauffmann called Hellman "the most overrated American dramatist of the century," as if her dramaturgy were in some way reflected in the film—which, of course, was not the case. The film contained the basic ingredients of Hellmann's plot, little of her dialogue, and none of her art.

One could readily understand if Hellman chose not to work in films again. Cinematically, the early 1960s were not kind to her; neither *The Children's Hour* nor *Toys in the Attic* was a success. Yet she was not averse to returning to screenwriting: "You can make a very good case for pictures being a lot better than the theater these days," she argued in a 1962 interview. Three years later, she was working on her sixth screenplay.

On paper, the project seemed to be a serendipitous combination of screenwriter, director, and producer: it would be the movie version of Horton Foote's 1952 play, *The Chase*, which Foote published as a novel four years later. Hellman would write the screenplay, and Arthur Penn, who had staged *Toys in the Attic* on Broadway, would direct. The producer would be Sam Spiegel, who won the Irving Thalberg Memorial Award in 1963 for the consistently high quality of his films, which included *The African Queen* (1951), *On the Waterfront* (1954), *The Bridge on the River Kwai* (1957), *Suddenly, Last Summer* (1959), and *Lawrence of Arabia* (1962).

Spiegel envisoned a film with assassination as a controlling but sunken metaphor; he wanted the climax to evoke President Kennedy's assassination without making any reference to it. Spiegel felt that if the subtextual meaning were sufficiently clear, audiences would associate the sudden and senseless killing of the protagonist with the slaying of Kennedy. He also believed that, in the mid 1960s, audiences would accept a film portraying an America whose amber waves of grain had been singed by the fires of violence. President Johnson had escalated the Vietnam war, and even men in the twenty-six to thirty-five age group were liable for the draft. The student uprising at Columbia University was two years away, but teach-ins were already beginning. It was the right time to take Horton Foote's parable of an escaped convict who returned to his Texas hometown only to be killed by a sheriff trying to save him from a lynching, and turn it into an allegory of an America that kills what it does not understand.

The Chase, as Spiegel conceived it, appealed to Hellman. Still in her *Toys in the Attic* mood, she was disposed to a work that did not portray man at his finest. Her latest play, *My Mother, My Father and Me*, satirized everyone and everything—nursing homes, youthful idealism, the younger generation and their elders. It was one of the first plays on Broadway to use "fuck," surpassing another Hellman first—"vagina" in *Toys in the Attic*. With the failure of *My Mother, My Father and Me*, the unsuccessful film versions of *The Children's Hour* and *Toys in the Attic*, and an undeclared war in southeast Asia, Hellman was ready to tackle *The Chase*. At the time, she did not know what she would be tackling.

The Chase existed in three forms: the 1952 play, the 1956 novel, and a 1959 draft of a screenplay that combined elements of the play and the novel with material taken from two of Foote's television dramas.

Horton Foote was one of the finest television playwrights of the golden age of the medium, that brief period in the 1950s when live drama was available virtually every night of the week and on Sunday afternoon as well. However, Foote's art was too fragile and small-scale for Broadway. He wrote *The Chase* in a whittled-down language that was deliberately prosaic and bare, without the folk rhythms of McCullers or Faulkner. On the surface, the play was a contemporary Western climaxing in a showdown between a sheriff and an escaped convict. Foote made the convict, Bubber Reeves, a scapegoat whose existence reminded the townspeople of their own worthlessness. One does not even know why Bubber was imprisoned; yet he has vowed to kill Sheriff Hawes who, like the marshal in the movies, deplores violence but ends up committing it. Gradually, one stops taking the play literally. There is no other choice; not only is too much left unexplained, but "chase" is repeated so frequently that it becomes a "lit. crit." phrase like "quest" and "odyssey"—words that induce a respectful silence.

By shaping the play in the form of a parable, Foote was forced to resort to symbolism, which was never his forte. Like other television playwrights who wrote for the stage, Foote excelled at characterization. In his finest work for the theater, *The Trip to Bountiful* (1953) and *The Traveling Lady* (1954), both of which originated as television drama, he wedded character to setting rather than to plot, so that the play became a native myth.

Foote was basically a regional dramatist, but in *The Chase*, he sacrificed setting and character to symbol. That he would rework the play as a novel four years after its Broadway failure was not surprising since the characters were so thinly spun. Hawes is the lawman who must eventually kill; Ruby is his loyal wife. Kim Hunter, a talented actress and the original Stella of *A Streetcar Named Desire* (1947), was given the impossible task of making Ruby interesting. She might have been had Foote developed the restlessness of which she speaks. When Ruby reveals her "hunger" to carry a child within her, one feels she could have been another earth mother like Abbie in O'Neill's *Desire under the Elms* (1924) or Serafina in Williams's *The Rose Tatoo* (1950). But Ruby Hawes is neither earthy nor maternal, but just a pregnant sheriff's wife.

Bubber's wife, Anna, was played by another fine actress, Kim Stanley, whose career began to wane in the early 1960s. Foote also gave her the bones of a character, although he implied there was flesh. When Anna yearns to witness a snake-handling ceremony, flesh starts closing over the bones, but not enough to create a bedeviled figure.

Bubber Reeves is the play's chief problem. His role is neither as large nor as dimensional as it should be. As scapegoat, Bubber must suffer for the sins of others. The town weakling, Edwin Stewart, stood by while Bubber was sent to reform school for a ten-dollar theft for which Stewart was responsible. Bubber seems to be persecuted not for what he is—we do not know what he is—but for what others are. To punish Bubber for his recalcitrance, his mother would dress him as a girl. Obviously, this was an extreme form of punishment unless Mrs. Reeves knew something we don't. Perhaps one should not ask too many questions of a scapegoat; but Horton Foote is too realistic a writer to leave questions unanswered, and not enough of an allegorist to satisfy us with a symbolic explanation when we need a literal one.

The Chase lasted for 31 performances on Broadway; it had a competent cast (John Hodiak, whose understudy was the then unknown Jason Robards, Murray Hamilton, Kim Stanley, Kim Hunter) and a talented director (José Ferrer). The 1956 novel fared slightly better; at least it attracted a few good reviews. But Foote had still not solved the basic problem, which was one of characterization. While the play tended toward thinness, the novel courted excess; it was a three-part narrative in 66 chapters running close to 300 pages. Thinking perhaps in terms of film rights, Foote added some minor characters—an unmarried daughter and her mother, a religious fanatic, a corrupt realtor—and in a series of vignettelike chapters, intercut their activities with the main action. Foote's other additions included a wife for Edwin Stewart by the name of Elizabeth; Elizabeth's lover, Hawks Damon; and Damon's wife, Minnie, a scatterbrain with a pistol fetish.

The play spanned a twenty-four-hour period, but Foote found it difficult to maintain unity of time in a novel with so much simultaneous activity. He therefore added retarding episodes, one of which was used in the film: a "Bubber Reeves" party that Damon organized on the pretext of protecting Elizabeth.

In the novel, the party was padding—an attempt to extend the fable into fiction. Bubber does not appear until Chapter 18, and while the bulk of the narrative covers a four-day period, the action itself comprises two years. It is the kind of novel in which one learns what happens to the characters; except for Hawes, who resigned as sheriff after Bubber's death, everyone else came back to the town. Yet the end of the novel has a strange power; only then does one realize what it might have been. The ending illuminates the nature of the clash between Bubber and Hawes. When Hawes fires repeatedly at Bubber, he is really killing the scapegoat within himself. With Bubber's death, Hawes can resign from a job he loathes and return to the soil. Bubber is Hawes's double, for he too wants deliverance—from life. "I'm whipped. I've got no fight left," Bubber tells his mother in one of the few moving episodes in the novel. Thus, when he walks toward Hawes, he is not even armed.

At the very end of the novel, one discovers that "Bubber" was only a nickname; his real name was Jackson, a venerable name, perhaps standing for the kind of democracy the townspeople could not accept. It is easier to persecute a Bubber than a Jackson.

In 1956, the year *The Chase* appeared as a novel, a collection of eight of Foote's television plays was published under the title *Harrison, Texas*. Sam Spiegel, who was not impressed by *The Chase* when he saw it on Broadway, saw possibilities in the novel as well as in two of the Harrison plays, *John Turner Davis* (1953) and *The Midnight Caller* (1953)—the former directed by Arthur Penn for Philco Television Playhouse. Apparently, Spiegel planned to combine material from the two television plays with *The Chase* to form one screenplay. It was probably for this reason that he bought the rights to *The Chase*, *John Turner Davis*, and *The Midnight Caller* at the same time.

Spiegel was ready to produce *The Chase* in 1959. A *Newsweek* notice (28 December 1959) mentioned that Spiegel was working on two films simultaneously—*Lawrence of Arabia* and *The Chase*, "a contemporary Western with moral overtones." In fact, a preliminary script of *The Chase* existed as early as March 1959. In the Margaret Herrick Library of the Academy of Motion Picture Arts and Sciences in Los Angeles, there is an anonymous screenplay of *The Chase* dated 11 March 1959 and labelled "first draft"; it is written in play form with "three major sequences, or acts, and an epilogue," and the setting is Harrison, Texas, the mythical town on the Gulf Coast that was the setting of the eight television plays and the novelization of *The Chase*.

The existence of this 1959 script with its strong similarities to the 1966 film proves it was the one from which Hellman worked when she became involved in the project in late 1964 or early 1965. (Spiegel's preoccupation with *Lawrence of Arabia* caused *The Chase* to be deferred for a few years.) Whoever wrote the preliminary script had forged a screenplay from the three Horton Foote works that Spiegel had purchased in 1956. The title character of *John Turner Davis* was a boy abandoned in Harrison by his aunt and uncle and adopted by a childless couple. At the end of the 1959 script, Hawes and Ruby, childless in this version, leave Harrison with John Turner Davis. In the television play, one never learns what happened to John Turner Davis's aunt and uncle, who were migrants. The 1959 script would have had the film open with their death in a car crash; the driver of the other car was to have been Bubber, who had just escaped from prison.

The Midnight Caller provided the anonymous screenwriter with a minor character, "Cutie" Spencer, and an important theme: rich boy / poor girl / meddling parent. The screenwriter merged the poor girl's character with Anna Reeves to create a convict's wife from the wrong side of the tracks. Harvey Weems, the rich boy of the television play, was the model for Jason (Jake) Rogers, the local tycoon's son and Anna's lover.

The real innovation, however, was the creation of a character out of a mere name. In the novel, Harrison is controlled by a shadowy triumvirate—Weems, Mavis, and Strachen. Weems never appears in the novel, but presumably he is the father of Harvey Weems of *The Midnight Caller*. Just as Harvey Weems became Jake Rogers, his father became Val Rogers, no longer an oligarch but an auto- crat who owns every major industry in Harrison. With the addition of Rogers, the script took on a political dimension. Rogers is a dynast who has carved an empire out of a Texas oil town. But it is an empire built on sterility—another theme that pervades the screenplay. Rogers has become sterile; in fact, he "barely begat Jason." Jason, who defies his father by becoming a liberal, needs Anna because she offers an escape from the sterility of affluence. She may be "common as dirt," but it is "rich fertile dirt."

While the author of the 1959 screenplay showed an ability to conflate sources and handle a political subtext, he or she had little sense of contrast. For the most part, the characters were unsympathetic. Good did not counterbalance evil because no one was good; and those who should not have been corrupt were. Sheriff Hawes and Rogers are close friends; Hawes does not even mind Rogers sending Ruby presents. Anna is the local slut who once even slept with Hawes, who, like everyone else in Harrison, loathes Bubber. The citizens of Harrison love a good bloodletting; when they learn that Bubber is hiding in the cottonwoods, they go "Bubber hunting." With the pistol party and the adultery between Damon and Elizabeth retained from the novel, it is hard to imagine a more unattractive group of people. The exception is Jason, who is killed while attempting to drive Bubber to safety; Hawes cuts him off, and the car plunges over the pier.

Credits give only the bald facts of a film. *The Chase* credits read: "Based on a Novel and Play 'The Chase' by Horton Foote. Screenplay by Lillian Hellman." However, unless one knew about the 1959 script, one would assume that Hellman was responsible for any changes in the original play and novel. For example, the film has a unity of time; so did the play, but not the novel. Without the facts, one could put up a good argument that Hellman created a unity of time by limiting the action to a single Saturday. One could cite as evidence Hellman's own work; the plays suggest continuous action even though none of them has the strict unity of time that characterizes Sidney Kingsley's *Detective Story* (1949). Still, *The Searching Wind* unfolds in one evening, and the time span of most of her plays rarely exceeds a few weeks; and in *Another Part of the Forest* and *Toys in the Attic*, the action is limited to a few days. But one would be wrong in crediting Hellman with *The Chase's* unity of time; it was determined in 1959 that the film would cover a twenty-four-hour period.

It would also be tempting to call Val Rogers an avatar of Ben Hubbard and regard the men who work for him as spin-offs of Oscar and Leo Hubbard. For the Hubbard analogy to work, one of the children in the dynasty must renounce riches—Zan in *The Little Foxes;* Jake Rogers in *The Chase*, who tries to compensate for his father's ways by treating the workers with respect. It is a plausible conjecture, but untrue. Hellman did not create Val Rogers and his son; they existed in the 1959 draft. In fact, except for the assassination motif, most of the main themes and all of the major characters were already present in the preliminary script.

One might ask, then, how Hellman received screenplay credit. The answer is simply by restructuring the first draft the way she restructured Frances Marion's scenario of *The Dark Angel* back in 1935. The first draft lacked contrast and balance; it was also overburdened by the John Turner Davis subplot. The boy is deleted, but the couples remain, most of them with different names. "Ruby" was right for the milieu, but "Hawes" was too redneck. Thus Hawes became Calder (Marlon Brando). Hawks Damon was a name suitable for a rock star, not a vice president in Val Rogers's bank. Hawks Damon became Damon Fuller, and his wife, Minnie, was renamed Mary. Emily (formerly Elizabeth) Stewart inherited Minnie's obsession with pistols.

But there was still an imbalance in the script. For the sake of symmetry, Jake Rogers needed a wife; Hellman supplied him with one, using Mrs. Stewart's former name—Elizabeth. She also provided a wife for the venal realtor, now called Briggs instead of Mavis. All of these couples are childless. Hellman made the sterility theme more pronounced than it was in the preliminary script. In fact, Val Rogers (E. G. Marshall) is so eager for progeny that he endows a college that bears his name, hoping to keep the youth of Tarl County from going elsewhere for an education.

The setting is now Tarl; it was Richmond in the play, Harrison in the novel. Perhaps it was thought that Tarl, the name of a deputy in the play, had an onomatopoeic quality ("tar," "snarl") suited to a community peopled by so many despicable types.

Gradually, the script was taking shape, but it still needed more contrast. Accordingly, Hellman made Rogers and Calder antagonists. Then she revived a plot device she had used in *The Dark*

Angel: she made the three principals—Jake (James Fox), Anna (Jane Fonda), and Bubber (Robert Redford)—childhood friends who form a rebel trio in defiance of Val Rogers. But it is an unusual trio, since Bubber is still the scapegoat that he was in the original. However, he is now a specific type of scapegoat: a Christ figure with Anna as the Magdalen and Jake as the beloved disciple.

Exactly whose idea it was to make Bubber a Christ figure is unclear. Theoretically, any scapegoat has the potential to become a sacrificial Christ; he need only be guiltless. In Bubber's case, there is a moral disparity between the crime and the punishment. He is serving a two-year prison sentence, but for what we are not certain; *perhaps* it was for stealing cars or flying an airplane while drunk. However, the community fears and hates him because he is a rebel and a free spirit in a town that is conformist and submissive. His mother beat him, and the town persisted in calling him by his childhood nickname, which seems the kind that originated in derision. Bubber's real name is Charlie, but only his father calls him that.

The true scapegoat resigns himself to death; or, to use Mary Renault's famous phrase in *The King Must Die* (1958), he must "go consenting." Bubber welcomes death: "I was coming to the end of me," he explains in his folk grammar. When a guard tried to force him to eat spoiled pork, he refused: "When you're willing to die, no one can make you do anything."

The film contains a major alteration in the scapegoat myth that makes Bubber's death an example of tragic waste rather than classic tragedy. Traditionally, the scapegoat is killed by the usurper or the new king; this is how the play and the novel concluded— with the killing of the convict by the sheriff. But Spiegel wanted a contemporary slant, one that would jolt the audience into a state of historical awareness.

When word gets out that Bubber is down at the junkyard near the wharf, the town turns out for the kill. The crowd is in a Dionysian mood, setting off firecrackers, sending up flares, and rolling burning tires down the incline into the ideal bombing site for the children's wargames, the junkyard where Bubber, Anna, and Jake are hiding. (To the town, the three of them are junk.) The flares that turn the sky inferno-red, the pools of burning gasoline, and the plate glass store that explodes into a spray of splinters cannot fail to evoke Vietnam; it is as if the war in southeast Asia had been transferred to the home front with makeshift bombs replacing napalm, and excited youngsters hurling firebombs aping the "zippo squads" of marines who set fire to Vietnamese peasant huts.

The ending was intended to suggest another historical parallel. Calder manages to rescue Bubber from the mob, but, on the steps of the county jail, Bubber is shot by one of Damon Fuller's drunken cronies. Most of the critics picked up the intended comparison between Bubber's assassination and other Texas assassinations— President Kennedy's and Lee Harvey Oswald's. While one assassination may recall another, Bubber's was not politically motivated; it was a senseless act of violence in a film portraying senseless acts of violence. Since the analogies with Kennedy and Oswald are tenuous, they should not be pressed. The film's basis is mythic. Bubber, who lived a scapegoat's life, dies a scapegoat's death, murdered by one embodying the corruption he despised. As his life ebbs away, he assumes a fetal position, his fingers curving inward like an animal's paws.

The Chase was not a happy experience for either Penn or Hellman. Penn has all but disowned it, but Penn has always overreacted to cuts and reediting. Robin Wood, who has written sympathetically of Penn's work, is not above calling him "the last person in the world to go to for an impartial view of what actually reached the screen."[2] What reached the screen was Sam Spiegel's vision of the script as executed by Hellman and Penn. Horton Foote, whom Spiegel brought in to "modify" Hellman's script, maintains that "the basic concept . . . is really Sam Spiegel's, not Lillian's. Sam had strong ideas about what he wanted, and she worked along these lines."[3] Foote, however, could not work along those lines "to my or his satisfaction."[4]

Yet neither Penn nor Hellman asked that their names be removed from the credits, as Mervyn Le Roy and George Cukor did as director(s) of *Desire Me* (1947), as Ernst Lubitsch did as producer of *Dragonwyck* (1946), and as Paddy Chayefsky did as screenwriter of *Altered States* (1981). Furthermore, the data form for the *Bulletin of Screen Achievement Records* (18 January 1966) lists Hellman as the sole screenwriter. No names are listed under

Marlon Brando as Sheriff Calder in *The Chase* **(1966).** *(Columbia Pictures Corporation)*

"other substantial contributors," who would be "writers whose contribution represented more than 10% of the value of the completed screenplay." As Hellman will admit, "most of the writing is mine,"[5] although, in the film, the scenes do not always appear in the order that she intended.

Spiegel was obviously a difficult man to please since *The Chase* was such a personal film for him. But it would seem that Hellman's main objection was to the way the film turned out. *The Chase* is not a writer's film; it is a film of images, some of which are memorable for their sheer flamboyance—for example, the apocalyptic climax—and others for their grossness: Val Rogers's birthday party, where a crone in a pink pantsuit dances the Jerk, bosoms burst out of bodices, and buttocks are so tightly girdled that they look like twin cushions. Visually, *The Chase* has the look of rainbow-colored rot. At times the screen is saturated with a white-streaked aquamarine, spectral and Dantesque, like vapors rising from the pools of the underworld. This kind of hellish lushness begins in the credits sequence, which Penn claims he did not shoot but which blends in so seamlessly with the film that one would never know it.

The Chase was poorly reviewed when it was released, but since 1966 it has come to be regarded as a key film of the 1960s—not as a major work of art, for it is clearly flawed, but as the summation of a period that might be called the decade of the scapegoat—the decade of John Kennedy, Robert Kennedy, Martin Luther King, the Vietnam war dead, the Kent State students. Viewed in this context, *The Chase* becomes a requiem, perhaps too loudly played but nonetheless deeply felt, for the slain of the sixties.

9

Footfalls in the Memory: *Julia*

In 1960, Lillian Hellman was a playwright; in 1969, she was a memoirist. The 1960s opened auspiciously for her, with the Broadway success of *Toys in the Attic* and a run of 464 performances. Three years later, there was the debacle of *My Mother, My Father and Me*, which barely lasted for 17.

By the early 1960s, Hellman had soured on the theater. But Hollywood had also changed, and her experience with *The Chase* left her with few illusions about the movie industry. For a playwright who had ruled out fiction early in her career, there were not many literary forms left that would suit her talent, except the memoir. She may have been thinking of the memoir when she edited *The Big Knockover* (1966), a collection of Hammett stories. Her introduction was a touching recollection of Hammett, which she later incorporated into *An Unfinished Woman*. The introduction also made it plain that if she could stir the waters of memory without clouding them, she might develop into something more than a memoirist; perhaps a chronicler like Malcolm Cowley, defining an era by delineating the figures who epitomized it.

Unfortunately, Hellman's style precluded her becoming a model autobiographer. The tautness of the plays made it even harder to accept the flabbiness of the memoirs with their polysyndetic prose ("and" recurs with childlike frequency) and the constant references to a poor memory ("I have no memory of . . ." is formulaic). Yet the first three memoirs—*An Unfinished Woman* (1969), *Pentimento* (1973), and *Scoundrel Time* (1976)—found favor with the public and with many critics. As a result, Hellman became a celebrity courted by feminists for her independence and admired by the young for her integrity. Although *An Unfinished Woman* won the National Book Award, most of the honors Hellman received during the 1970s were nonliterary. The New York University Alumnae Club voted her woman of the year in 1973, and in the same year the New Jersey branch of the American Civil Liberties Union recognized her "outstanding contributions to civil liberties." In 1974 she received honorary doctorates from Yale and New York University, and two years later an honorary degree from Columbia University. In 1976 she joined the ranks of the legends by posing in "what becomes a legend most"—a Blackglama mink. And at the 1978 Academy Awards she was accorded a standing ovation.

Hellman's second memoir, *Pentimento: A Book of Portraits*, immediately caught Hollywood's attention. Paramount opted for "Willy," Hellman's portrait of her great-uncle, but the project never materialized. However, it was "Julia" that really interested the studios. In July 1974, Columbia Pictures announced its intention to film "Julia" with Nicholas Roeg as director and Harold Pinter as screenwriter. But it was Twentieth Century–Fox that finally made *Julia* (1977).

Julia was one of those dream collaborations between director, screenwriter, and stars. It would be difficult to imagine anyone other than Fred Zinnemann as *Julia's* director; perhaps Wyler, although he had not made a film since *The Liberation of L. B. Jones* (1970). One could certainly not imagine the director Fox had originally announced—Sydney Pollack. Zinnemann's forte was the film of courage—political prisoners escaping from a German concentration camp (*The Seventh Cross*, 1944), a marshal deserted by his townspeople (*High Noon*, 1953), a subject who challenged his king (*A Man for All Seasons*, 1966). Zinnemann was a self-effacing director, in the sense that he could interpret a script without imposing his personality on it. There is an artistic anonymity about a Zinnemann film; unlike the work of an *auteur*, Zinnemann's work is unsigned.

Because his films do not abound in directorial touches and personal details, many find his work austere, particularly *Behold a Pale Horse* (1964), *The Nun's Story* (1959), and *A Man for All Seasons*. Zinnemann's so-called austerity is the result of emotion refined and sometimes withheld, so that the characters are not demeaned by sentiment or pity. The emotion is in the drama, but not in embellishments like plangent music or glycerine tears cascading down the heroine's face. Zinnemann's art is typified in the restrained parting of Burt Lancaster and Deborah Kerr in *From Here to Eternity* (1953). As they bid good bye, she looks up at him, shielding the sun from her eyes with her hand.

The screenplay for *Julia* was written by Alvin Sargent, who began his writing career in television and in the late 1960s turned to the movies, authoring the scripts of *The Sterile Cuckoo* (1969), *The Effect of Gamma Rays on Man-in-the Moon Marigolds* (1972), *Paper Moon* (1973), and *Bobby Deerfield* (1977). Eager to make *Julia* as authentic as possible, he immersed himself in Hellman's work. The fruits of his study are reflected in small but significant ways, such as the scene in which Lilly is at the typewriter trying to complete her first play. The dialogue she has typed is taken directly from *The Children's Hour*.

When the cast for *Julia* was announced, it seemed incredible that two leading actresses would be playing Lilly and Julia: Jane Fonda and Vanessa Redgrave, respectively. In the 1930s and 1940s, for a star of Redgrave's stature to appear in a supporting role would have meant the beginning of the end. Yet Redgrave won an Oscar for best supporting actress, as did Jason Robards (Dashiell Hammett) for best supporting actor. At first, one wonders why Hammett is in the film since he does not figure prominently in the original sketch. The reason for his presence, according to Zinnemann, was "to counterbalance Lillian's relationship with Julia, so that the latter would not appear to have a lesbian undercurrent."[1]

A commercial filmmaker cannot ignore mass psychology. However, a filmmaker of integrity can make a popular concession work to the movie's advantage. Hammett provided a counterbalance—and quite an effective one—but for reasons that have nothing to do with dispelling a potentially homosexual aura. Hammett acts as Lilly's editor; he is her literary conscience, in contrast to Julia, who is her moral conscience. Yet Hammett and Julia are also memories, and the film is as much a study of memory as it is of commitment and responsibility. *Julia* is more than the movie version of the third portrait in *Pentimento*; it is the essence of *Pentimento*. In fact, *Julia* begins with Lilly's off-camera voice reciting the *Pentimento* preface:

Old paint on canvas, as it ages, sometimes becomes transparent. When that happens, it is possible, in some pictures, to see the original lines: a tree will show through a woman's dress, a child makes way for a dog, a large boat is no longer on an open sea. That is called pentimento because the painter "repented," changed his mind. . . .

In the screenplay, Sargent retained the spirit of the memoir by recreating Hellman's distinctive way of remembering. To Hellman, the act of remembering is self-reflective rather than self-conscious. In recalling the past, the memoirist comments on it, noting its relation to what was and what is. The remembered event becomes the matrix of the narrative, but the perspective is the memoirist's. It is she who can see the event in terms of what preceded and followed, flashing back and forward in cinematic fashion, so that a 1937 train trip will have its antecedents in a complex of memories that began in 1920, and its consequences in the memorist's subsequent development as a woman and a writer.

In addition to being the best-written sketch in *Pentimento,* "Julia" is also proof that Hellman profited from her experiences as a screenwriter. "Julia" contains flash-forwards as well as flashbacks within a flashback. The story begins with Hellman's recalling a 1937 trip to Moscow during which she stopped off in Paris. There she was approached by Mr. Johann, a member of the anti-Nazi underground, who gave her a message from Julia requesting—but not demanding—that she transport money from Paris to Berlin.

At this point, another flashback starts to materialize; it is as if Hellman were filming the event, marking the beginning of a dissolve as the letter precipitates a slow return to the past. One can almost visualize Julia's handwriting becoming indistinct as the present fades out and the past fades in. This is exactly what happens. 1937 yields to the early 1920s: the Saturday nights Hellman spent at the New York mansion where Julia lived with her grandparents; the camping trips she and Julia took together; Julia's early awareness of social injustice; her decision to study medicine at Oxford; and her espousal of Socialism, which brought her to a commune in the Floridsdorf district of Vienna in the late 1920s.

Yet "Julia" is more than time remembered; it is time interpreted and reflected on. When reflecting, one tends to digress and associate freely. Thus, after Hellman recalls an incident with an acquaintance, Anne-Marie Travers, who had seen Julia in Vienna in the mid 1930s, she digresses on the time in a bar when she struck Anne-Marie's brother Sammy for alleging that her love for Julia was lesbian. One bar brawl recalls another, and Hellman digresses on one that occurred much earlier, when James Thurber threw a whiskey glass at her in a speakeasy.

The film reproduced the temporal disjunctions and fragmented narrative of the original; yet it also reproduced the context of the narrative. The context of "Julia" is *Pentimento*. The title is an art term meaning that the artist "repented" or changed his mind in mid painting, turning a tree into a person or a person into a tree. Thus in *Pentimento*, one is looking at outlines or sketches of people rendered impressionistically. To accomplish her task, Hellman turns off into the byways of memory even though such detours result in digressions and narrative breaks.

The situation is complicated by the fact that Hellman is both writing a memoir and telling a story that includes the standard elements of plot, character, and setting. Because Hellman is telling the "story" of Julia, the narrative has a fictive quality; it also has a plot twist. In the first paragraph, the reader learns that the father of Julia's child is "almost certainly" living in San Francisco. Midway in the narrative John Von Zimmer appears; he is Julia's elusive friend whom Hellman tried to locate in 1934 when she was in Vienna. Then, in 1936, Anne-Marie reenters Hellman's life; she is now married to one of Julia's acquaintances from her medical school days in Vienna—John Von Zimmer. Finally, in 1970, Hellman spots Anne-Marie in a San Francisco restaurant but cannot bring herself to ask Von Zimmer "the old question" that had been haunting her since 1934.

Sargent wisely omitted the Von Zimmer subplot which, however factual it might be, was more bizarre than ironic. Furthermore, in a film, it could obscure the narrative focus, which was the relationship between Julia and Lilly. Dramatically, their relationship is the core of the film; contextually, it is the core of a memory around which other memories cluster. Sargent is committed to portraying the relationship as Hellman the memoirist perceived it, which would be quite different from the way Hellman the playwright would have dramatized it. Memoirists are not bound by a poetics, nor do they structure their narrative to resemble the old dramatic triangle where events mount in a line of tension to the apex and then descend into a resolution. There are too many turnoffs in the inward journey, too many forks in the road for linearity.

Linearity is impossible without narrative progression, without a "rising action," to use the academic term. In "Julia," Hellman is constantly fragmenting the narrative as she recounts a 1937 incident that occupies the center of a concentric circle of memories. *Pentimento* reads like Petronius's *Satyricon,* where episodes are on the verge of becoming intelligible when they splinter off into ellipses. The same was true of *An Unfinished Woman;* the reader no sooner reaches 1937 than Hellman brings the narrative to a halt and starts quoting from her diary. It is as if she were attempting a collage of her life rather than rendering an account of it.

Hellman's memoirs may be engrossing, but one is not tempted to reread them. The plays, however, are another matter. One is constantly struck by the surgical stitching together of episodes, the unerring variations in rhythm, and the maturity of reflection, especially in *The Autumn Garden,* which seems wiser with each reading. The memoirs are written casually, disjointedly; one can scarcely believe they were revised as systematically as the plays. Of course, one cannot prune memory the way one can prune an overwritten scene or an overlong act; and Hellman's memory cannot withstand the slightest trimming. Besides, pruning is not the method Hellman has chosen; she does not want to recreate the past with an Aristotelian beginning-middle-end. She wants to recreate it as she remembers it; even more, she wants to comment on the process of remembering and the events she remembers.

As intriguing as the concept may sound, the end result is disappointing. The memoirs suffer from imprecision; the latest, *Maybe* (1980), reads like Pinter and Robbe-Grillet stripped of subtext and ambiguity and recycled for mass consumption. Like Pinter, Hellman wonders whether something occurred as she remembers it or whether what she remembers even occurred; like Robbe-Grillet, she squeezes time into a ball as if it were a plaything. "Julia" is less flawed than some of the other pieces; it is not art, but it contains the seeds of art. Written cinematically, it has within it the template of a major film. But it needed someone to take the random "that reminds me of" connections and the jumps in space and time, and raise them to a higher level—to the level of emotional association and temporal dislocation. This is what Zinnemann and Sargent have done.

The artistry of their film lies in the atomization of the narrative through complex movie techniques, such as overlapping sound and associative cutting, that make reminiscence an act of the creative imagination rather than sorting through what Hellman in *Maybe* calls "the piles of bundles and ribbons and rags." The difference between "Julia," the sketch, and *Julia*, the film, can be seen from the following outline:

"Julia"

A. Prologue (1973)
B. Main Narrative, I (1937)
   1. Introduction
   2. Flashback sequence (1918–36)
      (a) Hellman's first New Year's Eve with Julia (1918)
      (b) Girlhood and adolescence (1918–early 1920s)
      (c) Julia's departure for Oxford (1925)
      (d) Hellman's visit to Oxford (c. 1926–27)
      (e) Julia's departure for Vienna (1928)
      (f) Meeting with Anne-Marie Travers and her brother Sammy (c. 1929); Thurber flashback (time unspecified)
      (g) Montagelike exchange of letters with Julia (1929–34)
      (h) Trip to Paris and Vienna (1934)
      (i) Second meeting with Anne-Marie (1936)
         Flash-forward (1970)
C. Main Narrative, II (1937–38)
   1. Train trip from Paris to Berlin
   2. Meeting with Julia in Berlin
   3. Continuation to Moscow

D. Julia's death
E. Epilogue (1950)

Julia

	TIME FRAME	CONTEXT
Prologue	1962*	Lilly in boat, remembering
	dissolve to 1937	Memory of Paris train
	dissolve to 1934	Prologue ends
Sequence 1	1934	Lilly with Hammett on Long Island, trying to write play
	voice-over to 1920*	First New Year's Eve with Julia
	dissolve to c. 1922	Second New Year's Eve
	cut to c. 1925	Third New Year's Eve
	cut to 1934	Back at Long Island with Lilly at typewriter
Sequence 2	1934	Lilly and Hammett on Long Island
	voice-over to 1922*	Lilly and Julia at summer lodge
	voice-over back to 1934	Lilly and Hammett in bed
	voice-over to 1923*	Julia's departure for Oxford
	voice-over to 1925*	Lilly's visit to Oxford
	voice-over back to 1934	Lilly and Hammett in bed
Sequence 3	1934 with wordless flashback	Lilly in Paris
	to 1923 during hospital scene	Lilly's visit to hospitalized Julia in Vienna

Sequence 4	1934–37	Lilly's play produced
		Lilly becomes celebrity
		Invitation to Moscow
Sequence 5	1937	Meeting with Mr. Johann in Paris
	voice-over to 1922	Lilly's memory of attempt to cross ravine
	dissolve to 1937	Lilly applies for visa to stop off in Berlin and see Julia
Sequence 6	1937	Journey from Paris to Berlin
	dissolve to 1923	Julia and Lilly in Adirondacks
	dissolve back to 1937	Lilly on train
Sequence 7	1937	Reunion in Berlin
Sequence 8	1937	Continuation to Moscow
	voice-over to 1930	Memory of Sammy in bar
	cut back to 1937	Lilly on train
Sequence 9	1937	Lilly in Moscow
		Julia's murder crosscut with end of *Hamlet*
Sequence 10	1937	Lilly in London funeral parlor
	voice-over to 1922	Lilly and Julia in Adirondacks
Sequence 11	1937	Lilly's search for Julia's child
Sequence 12	1937	Lilly's return to America
		Attempt to see Julia's grandparents
		Conversation with Hammett with dissolve to Epilogue

Epilogue   1962   Lilly in boat
                                        Reminiscence
                                        completed

*Denotes dates in revised final script (20 September 1976). Sargent makes 1962, the year
after Hammett's death, the date of Lilly's reminiscence. His dates are slightly at odds with
Hellman's since he sets the first New Year's Eve in 1920. Hellman said she and Julia met
when both of them were twelve; thus their first New Year's Eve together would have been in
1918, not 1920. He also sets Julia's death in 1937, not 1938.

In "Julia," Hellman tried to link past and present in two chief
ways: fragmented narrative and free association which, unfortunately, she uses with less skill than other writers. Zinnemann and
Sargent have done cinematically what Hellman was unable to do
verbally: they supplied links that were imagistic and aural, inter-
lockings that were related thematically, and juxtapositions that
explained the present in terms of the past. But they had an additional problem. There is no physical setting for *Pentimento*, only
Hellman's memory. But a narrative film must be specific; the
memoirist must be remembering somewhere, some place.

Julia begins and ends with a shot of a solitary figure in a rowboat. Sargent is familiar not only with "Julia" but also with Hellman's other pieces in *Pentimento*. He has taken the opening image,
one of loneliness and isolation, from "Turtle," the penultimate
sketch in the memoir, where Hellman is alone in a rowboat on Lake
Tashmoo off Martha's Vineyard. The long shot of Lilly in the boat
dissolves into the water. The connection is fitting since the waters
of memory are being stirred. But a memory of what? Appropriately,
the next shot is of a train pulling out of a station. Zinnemann will
repeat that shot later on; it is the train departing from the Gare du
Nord, the train that brought Lilly from Paris to Berlin in 1937.
Although the significance of the train is not yet clear, it is the first
image to surface from the pools of memory. The initial image has a
narrative importance since the train trip is the most dramatic part
of the film. The train dissolves into the water, and superimposed
over the surface are a pair of eyes seared by time. They are Lilly's
eyes peering through the water as a year begins to emerge from the
depths: 1934, when she was living with Dashiell Hammett and
trying to finish *The Children's Hour*.

As she struggles with the play, the voice of the mature Lilly is heard in counterpoint with her younger self. The older Lilly is struggling not with words but with memories, particularly her memory of Julia, the one memory she trusts "absolutely." The mention of Julia's name evokes Julia herself, and the action slips back to a New Year's Eve dinner at the home of Julia's grandparents. The first shot of the young Julia reveals a twelve-year-old pre-Raphaelite beauty, but without the ethereal reserve of a Rossetti damsel. Julia must have an aura that makes Lilly stand in awe of her, but also a fervor that would lead her to the slums of Vienna to live and work among the poor.

Everything Julia will reject appears in the dinner sequence. In an establishing shot, the grandparents sit at opposite ends of a table that stretches the length of the frame. Shots of beef meticulously sliced, the skeleton of a fish that had been impeccably boned, and sherbert served between the courses to clear the palate delineate a world where wealth produces surfeit, and surfeit, boredom. Julia could never belong to such a world; her renunciation of her family's materialism makes one think of saints like Jerome Emilian and Elizabeth of Hungary who shared their wealth with the less fortunate, or the radicals who came from affluence and wanted an equal distribution of wealth because they had seen how a few monopolized it.

In *Julia*, the plot advances through narrative fragments made up of dialogue and voice-over or images linked by association. Thus it is not a film that can be absorbed in a single viewing. Like *Citizen Kane* (1941) and *Hiroshima Mon Amour* (1960), which it resembles in its segmented chronology, *Julia* relies as much on dialogue as on *mise-en-scène* for its meaning. Sometimes the action unfolds through dialogue (the train sequence, the reunion of Lilly and Julia), sometimes through a modicum of dialogue and a preponderance of images (the dinner sequence, Julia's death).

Zinnemann crosscuts a performance of *Hamlet* that Lilly is attending in Moscow with Julia's assassination in Frankfurt. The result is a compelling form of emotional montage where a theatrical event and an actual occurrence are brutally juxtaposed. But Zinnemann is not merely contrasting a real tragedy with a staged one; he attempts to extract as much irony as he can from their juxtaposition by synchronizing Julia's murder with *Hamlet's* bloody climax. Applause begins just as the scene is about to change from the apartment where Julia was slain to the theater. Naturally, it is applause for the performance, but because it begins prematurely, one also associates it with the self-satisfaction Julia's assassins felt after the deed.

The crosscutting owes something to *Citizen Kane*. After Susan Alexander sings for Kane the first time, he applauds. The applause spills over into the next scene, but it is not for Susan; it is for Leland, who is campaigning for Kane. In both instances, applause bridges two distinct events that seem to be occurring simultaneously but obviously are not.

The collapsing of time in *Julia* also recalls *Citizen Kane*, where, in one scene, the young Kane says, "Merry Christmas" to his guardian; and in the next, the guardian says, "Happy New Year"—twenty years later. Similarly in *Julia*, after the New Year's Eve dinner, the girls go to Julia's room and, at the stroke of twelve, wish each other a happy New Year. Cut to Lilly and Julia celebrating another New Year's Eve a few years later, lying on the bed and improvising a mildly risqué story which each keeps embellishing until there is nothing more to add. In the next scene it is New Year's Eve again. The camera pans from the fireplace, right of frame, to Julia and Lilly on the floor, drinking wine and smoking cigarettes. They are young women now. Repeating their improvisation, they laugh at the suggestiveness they once thought so adult. After they toast the New Year, Julia's face remains left of frame in a transcendent close-up. The action slowly returns to 1934. Lilly is back at her typewriter, musing on the beauty of Julia's face, which has provided such an aesthetic transition.

One might expect a film like *Julia* to depict time subjectively, as an aggregate of images and memories existing outside space. However, Zinnemann refrains from doing anything quite so abstract. *Julia* is more concerned with memory than with time. Thus it contains nothing as pretentious as the chronological confusion of *Last Year at Marienbad* (1962). In *Julia*, time is rendered in terms of two popular metaphors: a pool to be dredged and an echo chamber to be entered.

In each case, a common proleptic device is used: overlap, in

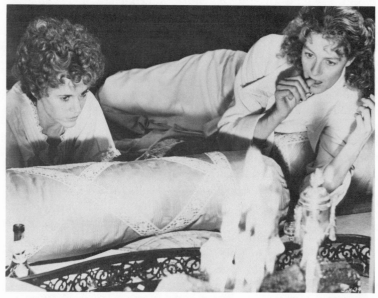

The young Lilly (Jane Fonda) and Julia (Vanessa Redgrave) celebrating New Year's Eve in *Julia* **(1977).** *(Twentieth Century–Fox Film Corporation)*

which the end of one scene anticipates the beginning of the next by means of dialogue or sound (such as music or noise) originating at the end of the first scene but belonging properly to the second. In *Julia*, overlap is not a gimmick but a mode of memory. Often we recall an incident in the form of a few isolated words, images, or sounds, which, as we search our memory, begin to weave a scenario of their own. But it is a scenario that originates in fragments—a snatch of dialogue, a noise, a picture.

For the most part, the overlap in *Julia* is successful. Early in the film, Lilly is having problems writing her play. As she lies down on the bed, one hears an offscreen voice asking, "What about Paris? What about Rome?" At this point, the context is unclear, but in a few moments the same dialogue will be repeated in the appropriate setting. The voice belongs to the young Lilly; the occasion, a vacation at Julia's summer lodge in 1922 when Lilly inquired about the various cities her friend had visited. But Julia was never a tourist; she was already a Socialist. In Cairo, she did not see the pyramids, but only the beggars; in Rome, not the Sistine Chapel but the slums. "It's wrong," she protested to Lilly.

Just prior to the train sequence, Lilly ponders something Julia had told Mr. Johann about her: that she was "afraid of being afraid." As Lilly walks through the Tuileries, an offscreen voice calls, "You don't have to come this way. Go down under. Wade across." Zinnemann intercuts Lilly's return to her hotel with another childhood experience, the time she tried to walk across a fallen tree that bridged a ravine, only to lose her balance and be rescued by Julia. However, it is not a single flashback but a fragmented one, suggesting the piecemeal way one faces the less pleasant aspects of childhood—not en masse but in segments. The flashback, which does not appear in the original, is nevertheless dramatically appropriate and provides a good illustration of how a reference, "afraid of being afraid," can be imaginatively visualized. As Lilly apologizes to Julia for being foolhardy, the past gives way to the present. Lilly is at the German embassy applying for a transit visa so she can stop off in Berlin and perform an act of humanity, not bravado.

After her meeting with Julia, Lilly continues on to Moscow. In her compartment, as she reflects on her friend, a disapproving voice remarks, "She's turned into a wild Socialist." The present dissolves to 1930 as Sammy Travers repeats the same line to Lilly in a bar.

There is one instance where overlap weakened the dramatic impact. When Lilly bends over Julia's body in a London funeral parlor, a girl's voice is heard saying, "I see a gun." The voice is Julia's, and the occasion was a camping trip in the Adirondacks. One might argue that there is a historical irony in the juxtaposition of girls playing a war game and a woman killed by the Nazis on the eve of a global war. Yet the effect is too portentous. The moment is too personal for history. Here Sargent might have followed Hellman and just used voice-over to convey Lilly's thoughts. For Hellman did not conceal what she felt for Julia. When she was alone with the corpse, looking down at the face that had been slashed by an assassin's knife, she wanted to give Julia the kiss in death that she had withheld in life. But she did not because she felt that, even now, Julia would not want it. The love Lilly bore for Julia went beyond friendship; it was the love of the knight for the lady. Julia quoted the classics while Lilly could recite only Mother Goose.

It might have made more sense if an earlier flashback on the train had been deferred until the funeral parlor scene. During the train ride, Lilly gazes out of the window, which becomes a screen on which the present fades out and the past fades in. The transition is punctuated by the sound of the locomotive transporting us to the past—to a campfire where Julia is reciting Herrick to an enraptured Lilly. When she finishes, Lilly says adoringly, "I love you, Julia." It is also the sound of the locomotive that brings us back to Lilly's compartment. Because the campfire flashback portrayed Lilly's awe for Julia with such tender yearning, it would have been more effective in the funeral parlor.

Hellman was dissatisfied with *Julia*, claiming that she had not expected to be portrayed as herself. She may also have thought the film was too "fancy," to use one of her favorite pejoratives. Understandably, she has always been happier adapting her own work than seeing someone else do it. Yet the film was, in its way, as honest as the memoir. The memoir was written in prose so ingenuous it could not possibly have been feigned; the film was made with a professionalism that turned ingenuousness into art.

Despite *Julia's* visual elegance, the performances of Fonda and Redgrave never allowed the audience to lose sight of the human drama that was at the heart of the film. Fonda's Lilly is the best work she has done thus far on the screen. She was called upon to do something Bette Davis and Olivia de Havilland did at the peak of their careers—appear in different stages of life. It was even more difficult for Fonda than it would have been for an actress in a 1940s film, where there were flashbacks but not fragmentation. Fonda sustained a character that was constantly being segmented and did it with none of the inconsistencies that often result when the star gains weight, loses her accent, or undergoes a personality change in the interval between youth and age.

At the heart of the memoir was the train trip, the best-written section in any of Hellman's autobiographical works, because it gave her an opportunity to do what she does best: to reduce character to dialogue and life to drama. It was written in language of effortless simplicity, much of which Sargent incorporated into his screenplay; it was also flavored with some good-natured humor that revealed one of Hellman's most endearing traits: her ability to laugh at herself. There is something wonderfully comic about the way Lilly becomes a courier for the anti-Nazi underground. One is forced to smile at the sheer incongruity of Lilly, dressed in an evening gown and a fur wrap, buying breakfast at the Hotel Meurice for an unshaven Socialist.

Mr. Johann instructed Lilly to greet him with a "hello" at the Gare du Nord if she would carry the money. Flustered, Lilly repeats "hello" so many times it could have been disastrous. When she enters her compartment, two women passengers, also members of the underground, must continually coach her. A second note told Lilly that the money was in a sealskin hat that she is to wear and a candy box that she is to leave in the compartment when she goes through customs at the German border. One of the women has to prod Lilly into opening the hat box. "You would put on," she tells Lilly with a hint of urgency in her voice. At the border, Lilly automatically picks up the candy box and must be reminded to leave it on the seat. As a secret agent, Lilly is a failure; as a human being, she is a complete success.

Humanity of a different type suffuses the meeting between Lilly and Julia and epitomizes Zinnemann's art of emotional restraint. Julia is sitting at a table at the far end of a café. With a wave of her hand, she beckons to Lilly. It is more than just a gesture of camaraderie. It is an expression of the sincerity that comes with tranquillity. In her work, Julia has found the "peace which passeth all understanding." Thus her welcome is not a frenetic wave of the arm to which those resort who think the measure of love is gush; rather, it is the arching of the arm to draw the other into a circle of love.

For her Julia, Redgrave deservedly won the Oscar for best supporting actress. She created a woman of education and breeding who found among the working classes what she could never find with her own kind: an identification with the human condition. In the underground, Julia discovered the freedom won by commitment. For, as Sartre noted, one is never freer than when there is danger of death. Yet Julia knows the movement is not for everybody; she is not the type of revolutionary who expects her friends to risk their lives for her cause. Her letter to Lilly is not a demand but a request; "no dishonor" if the request cannot be granted. Guilt does not exist in Julia's world; hence there is no possibility of her inflicting it on Lilly.

There are no tears in Julia's world, either. When Lilly notices her artificial leg, Julia anticipates her reaction: "No tears, Lilly!" With a luminous air of acceptance that is neither stoic nor self-effacing, Redgrave magnificently portrays Julia's being-for-others. Dressed like a worker in a tweed jacket, green sweater, and skirt, Redgrave's Julia also talks like one. Unlike many British actresses, Redgrave could affect an American accent without sounding artificial. In *Isadora* (1969), she flattened her a's until they were democratized. However, in *Julia*, she must sound like an American who has been living abroad for more than a decade and who has become a bilingual Socialist. Julia, who once awed Lilly by quoting French, Latin, and Italian poetry, now lapses into slang. When she speaks of her baby, she remarks that Europe "ain't for babies these days."

When it is time to part, Julia, like the women on the train, must give Lilly her instructions. "Put the hat on, Lillian. Leave! Leave!" It is interesting to speculate on how many playwrights received stage directions from their characters.

10

The Significance of *Julia*

All we know about Julia is what Hellman has told us. Julia was her childhood friend, whose name she will not reveal. Her father was a Detroit millionaire, her uncle, a governor. Julia was raised by her grandparents, who were more interested in her fortune than in her. She had a fabled childhood: summers in the Adirondacks, trips to Rome and Cairo. Her life was short; she must have been in her early thirties when she was killed by Nazis.

The rest is conjecture. She and Hellman may have attended Waldleigh High School together in New York, from which Hellman was graduated in 1922. Perhaps Julia was the friend with whom she went spy-hunting along Riverside Drive in 1917, looking for German agents and mistaking a Hunter College classics professor for one. If so, it was a rehearsal for Hellman's exposure to espionage twenty years later.

Some of Hellman's detractors have denied that there ever was a Julia. The charge is never made so blatantly, but the implications are unmistakable. When Mary McCarthy appeared on the Dick Cavett Show in January 1980, she charged Hellman with being a "dishonest writer," whose every word is "a lie, including 'and' and ʿe.' "[1] McCarthy's animosity toward Hellman is part of a much ʿer antagonism that views her plays as melodramatic, her ʿ as intractably left-wing, her memoirs as unreliable, and ʿrial dependence on Hammett as proof that he was her ʿ on the plays.[2]

ʿbacklash, the stripes overlap. Thus, if one regards ʿ as examples of "oily virtuosity," as Mary McCar-ʿ be inclined to think similarly of the memoirs; ʿlman's politics offensively left-wing, one will ʿ work of "Socialist realism," as Elizabeth

Hardwick did in her review of the 1967 revival, while a more temperate critic would have used the term "social realism." It is doubtful that Anatoli Lunacharsky, who originated the term "Socialist realism," would have found *The Little Foxes* revolutionary.

Hardwick was at least specific about what she disliked in Hellman; McCarthy, on the other hand, was bluntly general: "I've never liked what she writes."[3] But the reason she gave had nothing to do with literature. It seemed that, in 1948, McCarthy overheard Hellman telling some students at Sarah Lawrence College that John Dos Passos had betrayed the Spanish Loyalists: "I couldn't stand this woman brain-feeding these utterly empty, innocent minds, and thinking she could get away with it."[4] Presumably Hellman told them that Dos Passos was supposed to collaborate with Hemingway and Joris Ivens on *The Spanish Earth* until he came disillusioned by the conduct of the Communist Loyalists. Whether she told the students the reason for his disillusionment is another matter. When Dos Passos arrived in Valencia, he heard that his friend, José Robles Pazos, had been arrested for treason; in Madrid, he discovered that Robles had been executed, apparently by the Communists.

It is not surprising that the Spanish Civil War played such an important factor in McCarthy's dislike of Hellman, for it was a war that had the same polarizing effect on intellectuals as Vietnam had three decades later. Hellman's position was unequivocal: an antifascist supports the Loyalists. It was not an uncommon view. Anyone in doubt could look to Auden, who, in *Spain* (1937), resolved the Loyalist-Nationalist dilemma: "I am your choice, your decision; yes, I am Spain." McCarthy made her own decision; she would not unilaterally support the Loyalists because of the Stalinist faction within the Loyalist ranks.

Stalinism was another source of contention between the two women. After the Moscow purge trials, McCarthy became an anti-Stalinist, while Hellman did not, although she was in Moscow the time and later chided herself for being so oblivious to the tri In *Scoundrel Time*, she also admitted her blindness to the "si Stalinism, which "for a long time [she] mistakenly denied." I Stalinist, one means someone who signed a statement sup the purge trials, as Hellman did in *The Daily Worker* (28 April 1938)—along with Hammett, Nelson Algren, Malcolm Cowley, Richard Wright, Langston Hughes, and others—then, naturally, she was. But such an endorsement should be viewed as the act of a hard-line Popular Fronter who steadfastly avoided criticizing the Soviet Union because it was the declared enemy of fascist aggression. To go any further and think of Hellman as a believer in gulags and the exiling of dissidents is to misinterpret a position that came out of a historical context. Even Sidney Hook, her fiercest critic, agrees she is no longer a Stalinist, although he seems to want a formal recantation of the sort the Inquisition demanded of heretics.

Had Hellman never written *Scoundrel Time*, one doubts that her critics would have raked up the coals of the past, searching for embers. Rarely has such a slender book occasioned such controversy. The prose was unadorned, although not as colorless as it was in *An Unfinished Woman*. The pacing suggested that Hellman had not lost her dramaturgical gifts. Yet unless one equates reminiscence with hagiography, *Scoundrel Time* is not "the record of a virtually unique personal heroism" that Diana Trilling claims it is.[5] To call it such is to detract from the true hero, Joseph Rauh, Hellman's attorney, but for whom she would never have written her famous letter to the House Committee on Un-American Activities and quoters would have lost one of Bartlett's best.

Nor was there anything especially heroic about Hellman's testimony, which is not recorded in *Scoundrel Time*. Compared with Lionel Stander's buffoonery and John Howard Lawson's moral rage, Hellman's responses were rather dull. She became so rattled that she took the Fifth Amendment when she did not have to, implying that at one time she was a Communist although she never belonged to the party.

The Hellman who emerges from *Scoundrel Time* is a woman subject to fear and anger as well as a woman in need of reassurance, which she certainly did not get from Hammett, who thought she might be going to jail and spent the evenings telling her about the rats that scamper about the cells. Regardless, Hellman stood by her letter and refused to name names; it was an action that should never be minimized, not because it was heroic but because it was human. Integrity is not heroism; it is clearly within a mortal's capabilities. Yet a third of the mortals who appeared before the House Committee lost their integrity.

Integrity is also not the prerogative of martyrs and saints, although no one would know it from Garry Wills's introduction, which Philip Dunne called "a piece of imaginative fiction worthy of a Pulitzer Prize."[6] The introduction did not help Hellman, nor did the action taken by her publishers, Little, Brown, who regarded *Scoundrel Time* as such a sacred text that they demanded that Diana Trilling delete four unfavorable references to Hellman from *We Must March My Darlings* before they would publish it. When Mrs. Trilling refused, Little, Brown terminated her contract.

Mrs. Trilling had no difficulty finding another publisher, yet when one reads those supposedly inflammatory passages, one wonders why Little, Brown went to such lengths to protect Hellman, who has always managed to weather personal and professional attacks, unless they expected *Scoundrel Time* to make her a national monument, which they did not want one of their own authors to deface.

Actually, Mrs. Trilling revealed nothing about Hellman that was not known. Even her discussion of Hellman's politics, while lucidly written, tells us more about the author as an anti-Communist liberal than it does about Hellman, who took another of her unequivocal stands during the McCarthy era—a stand that reflected a Popular Front mentality with McCarthyism replacing fascism. To Hellman, opposing McCarthyism meant opposing anti-Communism, which, in effect, meant being anti-anti-Communist. But to the right, a double negative was still a positive. The anti-Communist liberals did not have that problem. One could be anti-Communist and anti-McCarthy without the risk of being branded a Red.

Finally, to call *Scoundrel Time* an "unreliable history of the McCarthy era," as Mrs. Trilling does, is to misunderstand what the book really is: one individual's account of an event in which she participated. *Scoundrel Time* is to the history of McCarthyism what Edith Hamilton's *The Greek Way* is to the study of Hellenism: a primer, an introduction. What the memoir succeeded in portraying, and quite vividly, was an America under a kind of moral quarantine, where the illness was not severe enough to be an epidemic but only bothersome and nasty, like a prolonged case of flu that weakens the spirit and leaves the body smelling of flannel.

Yet the charge of unreliability is one that continues to haunt Hellman. Unlike the plays, which were often meticulously re-searched, the memoirs took an impressionistic view of history that would understandably infuriate anyone who wants a memoir to resemble a ship's log, with a strict correlation of date and event. One can appreciate Martha Gellhorn's exasperation at Hellman's seemingly cavalier attitude toward dates, especially since Gellhorn was a former war correspondent and journalist. Naturally one can respect Gellhorn's insistence on factual accuracy. But Hellman was not aiming for factual accuracy in her memoirs; she was seek-ing the essence of the event. To her, chronology was not the es-sence of the past, only one of its accidents. While it might seem laudable of Gellhorn to emend Hellman's chronology, she was not acting entirely in the interest of historical truth.

Tired of apocrypha about Hemingway and the Spanish Civil War, Gellhorn drew on newspaper accounts as well as her own experiences as the third Mrs. Ernest Hemingway and as a war correspondent who was in Spain at the same time as Hellman—in the fall of 1937.[7] Although she is occasionally persuasive in point-ing out discrepancies between Hellman's dates and the actual events, far too often she calls to mind the senior professor who sets out to demolish the thesis of a junior colleague by marshaling such an array of evidence that one begins to question the motive. What Gellhorn keeps forgetting is that Hellman is not writing history, and that what might be reprehensible to a journalist might not be to a literary critic. One can call the memoirs imprecise or say that they have the elliptical quality of a screen treatment as opposed to a finished screenplay; one can call the diary entries inaccurate or think of them as a collage of impressions rather than a record of events.

Sometimes Hellman is vague because she does not remember; sometimes her vagueness is deliberate. The visit to Spain and the trip to Berlin took place within the same time period. Since Hell-man has gone to great lengths to conceal Julia's identity, she may be using an inconsistent chronology to confound the curious. In *An Unfinished Woman*, she gave the name of Alice to the friend who became Julia in *Pentimento*, stating that she died in 1934, which became 1938 in the second memoir.

Nor is it an earth-shattering revelation to discover that Hellman's dating is sometimes off by a year. In *Scoundrel Time*, she gave the date of her divorce from Arthur Kober as 1931, although it was a year later. A Freudian might argue that it was because Hellman was born a year later than the records indicate—in 1906, not 1905. Even Garry Wills seems to have picked up the habit, citing 1944 as the release date of *Song of Russia* when it was the previous year.

Therefore, Hellman's statement that Hemingway brought a print of *The Spanish Earth* to Hollywood in 1938 is not the whopper that Gellhorn imagines it is. Obviously it was 1937, since the film was released in August of that year. Yet to say, as Gellhorn does, that Hellman could not have been present at "Hemingway's only showing of the film in Hollywood" is incorrect. Hellman claims she saw the film at the home of Fredric and Florence March, and there is no reason to doubt her word: "In the summer of 1937, Hemingway and Ivens brought *The Spanish Earth* to Hollywood. . . . The screenings—at Fredric March's home, at Salka Viertel's house, at the Ambassador Hotel, and in the Philharmonic Auditorium—brought in more than $35,000 for the cause."[8]

"But memory for us all is so nuts," Hellman observed rather prosaically in *Maybe*. Still, she knew *The Spanish Earth* was screened in the summer of 1937 and told Andrew Turnbull about it in the late 1950s when he was researching his biography of Scott Fitzgerald. Hellman, therefore, must have met Hemingway before "those pre-Moscow Paris weeks" in 1937 that she describes in *An Unfinished Woman*. However, she anticipates any criticism of her chronology by invoking her memory that sometimes "won't supply what I need to know," as she admits candidly in *Maybe*.

If the intent of Gellhorn's argument was to show that Hellman had no talent for reportage, one would agree. Yet as well researched as Gellhorn's piece is, it seems to be another chapter in the humbling of Hellman. Interspersed among the documentation are references to Hellman the "important lady" whose *An Unfinished Woman* reads like a novel and whose *Pentimento* reads like short stories. Twice, she quotes a sentence from "Julia," once italicizing it in disbelief: "But I trust absolutely what I remember about Julia."

Gellhorn ends her corrigenda by admitting she has many more questions about Hellman's accuracy, and even about "Julia." There is much one would like to know about Julia, but demanding personal and historical vindication will not lead to an understanding of the woman who was the model for many of Hellman's characters. And regarding Hellman as a Stalinist will make one even more skeptical that such a person ever existed. In the same essay in which he expressed doubts about the truthfulness of "Julia," Clive James called Hellman "an unreconstructed and unrepentant Stalinist," the assumption being that repentance and rehabilitation might make an honest writer of her. Instead, "the Julia chapter, like all the others, happens in a dream" and ultimately "rings false."[9]

It is one thing to say, as the *Times Literary Supplement* reviewer did in the context of a favorable notice, that "Julia" resembles a film scenario; it is something else to say, as James did, that it reads "like a spy-sketch by Nichols and May." For the moment, let us take a tabula rasa approach to Hellman, putting aside the image of Hellman the imperious doyenne whose face with its bisecting lines looks like the map of some uncharted land.

The land can be charted, and one might start with James's spy-sketch comparison. Certainly "Julia" has the ingredients of a spy thriller, and the role Lilly is required to play conjures up incidents in Eric Ambler, Graham Greene, and Helen MacInnes. Anyone who knows the thriller only from television or the movies would even sense something familiar about "Julia." By reducing the entire experience to a *pentimento* or an outline, Hellman has universalized it. If Lilly and Julia seem familiar, it is because one has seen them before in other incarnations. Lilly is the innocent drawn into a circle of intrigue; the lady on a train making a perilous journey. Julia is the radical who rejects the affluence from which she came; the saint from the privileged class who elects to serve the poor without desire for recognition. Unwilling to be styled a heroine, Julia will not allow others to playact at being heroic. In her second note to Lilly, Julia dashes any hope of recognition Lilly may have: "There is no thanks for what you will do for them. . . .

But there is the love I have for you." Julia has achieved total freedom from the nothingness of being-for-itself. Therefore, she evokes similarly committed women like Joan of Arc, Edith Cavell, Edith Stein, and Odette Churchill.

But Julia also evokes classical rebels like Prometheus and Antigone, and it is this archetypal link that makes her seem mythic. By spinning a narrative around Julia, Hellman has enclosed her within a myth—a truth that has been imaginatively universalized. However, as Suzanne K. Langer observed in *Philosophy in a New Key* (1948), myths are contradictory, as opposed to fairy tales, which remain simplistic. In one version of the Atreus myth, for example, Iphigenia is sacrificed by her father, Agamemnon; in another a stag is substituted for her, and Iphigenia goes off to Tauris. Hence, one should not be surprised to find inconsistencies in Julia.

In *An Unfinished Woman*, Hellman recalls a childhood friend called Alice, a millionairess who turned to Socialism and died in 1934 during the violence that erupted in February of that year when Engelbert Dollfuss, the right-wing chancellor of the Austrian Republic, closed Parliament and put down the protest strikes of the Viennese Socialists. Hellman would have been in Europe at that time, staying in Paris at the Hotel Jacob, where she was trying to complete *The Children's Hour*. In an incident common to both the memoir and the film, Hellman learned that her friend was hospitalized in Vienna. When Hellman arrived at the hospital, she found her friend speechless and almost completely wrapped in bandages.

Clearly Alice and Julia are the same person, whose identity Hellman simply will not divulge. It is also possible that in 1969, when Hellman published *An Unfinished Woman*, she had no plans of continuing her friend's story or of using it as the basis of a memory piece. A few years later, when she was ready to publish her second memoir, she decided otherwise; and so the friend who died as Alice in 1934 is given four more years of life.

Thus far we have been speaking of the mythico-historical Julia of the memoir; but there is also the Julia figure of the plays. Hellman was fascinated by the name of Julia. It was her mother's name, yet Hellman favored her father's side of the family. Hellman's mother was a Newhouse, and the Newhouses, as Hellman conceded, were the model for the predatory Hubbards of *The Little Foxes* and *Another Part of the Forest*. But the Hellmans were different. It was from her father that Hellman learned what it meant to be a liberal and to believe in racial equality, feeling so close to blacks that once, when she ran away from home, she wandered into a black ghetto and claimed she was related to her nurse, Sophronia Mason. The Newhouses, on the other hand, merely thought blacks had a distinctive odor. Julia Newhouse was the exception: "She was the only middle class woman I have ever known who has not rejected the middle class," Hellman wrote of her mother in *An Unfinished Woman*. Julia Newhouse found God everywhere and in everyone; in synagogues and cathedrals, in blacks and whites. Spiritually, she was a Julia—one of several.

In her very first play, *The Children's Hour*, Hellman transferred the homoerotic feelings she had for Julia, "the sexual yearning of one girl for another" as she phrased it in the memoir, to Martha, with Karen and Martha becoming the tragic counterparts of Lilly and Julia. Other details in *The Children's Hour* corroborate what Hellman has written in her memoir. In the play, a child accuses her teachers of lesbianism; in "Julia," Sammy Travers makes a similar allegation about Lilly and Julia. Hellman was in Vienna early in 1934 when Julia was hospitalized; in *The Children's Hour*, which premiered in November 1934, Joe Cardin offered to take Karen and Martha to Vienna, where he studied medicine. In *These Three*, Hellman supplied a happy ending for Julia's story. Learning that Joe is in Vienna, Karen goes there and is reunited with him. If life imitated the movies, Lilly and Julia would have enjoyed a similar reunion in Vienna.

In her second play, *Days to Come*, Julie Rodman, the wife of an industrialist, has an affair with a labor organizer. Julie embodies some of the more superficial features of the Julia figure: she is widely traveled, well bred, and wealthy. But intrinsically, Julie Rodman is more like Hellman. Like the young Hellman, whom Julia thought of as a student rather than a teacher, Julie Rodman was always searching for "something I could be" and for "somebody to show me the way." In *An Unfinished Woman*, Hellman confessed a similar desire: "I needed a teacher, a cool teacher. . . ."

In *The Little Foxes* screenplay, Hellman added a character called Julia. In a scene written especially for the film, Alexandra (Zan) finds the elegant Julia dining with David Hewitt and becomes jealous because she is interested in him herself. Zan is a composite of Julia and Hellman. Like Julia, she rebelled against her family's avarice; like Hellman, who once charged her family with being immoral when she was going through her righteous phase, Zan accused the Hubbards of "eating the earth."

Watch on the Rhine was a blueprint for "Julia." In the play, Kurt Müller carried $23,000 in a briefcase, not unlike Lilly, who carried $50,000 in a hat and a candy box. Both Kurt and Julia bear the scars of commitment. Kurt's face is bullet-marked, and the bones in his hands have been broken; during the Vienna riots, Julia, in addition to being badly beaten, lost a leg.

In *The North Star*, the Nazis tortured Sophia by breaking her arm and leg. At the end of *The Searching Wind*, Sam Hazen was about to lose a leg because of injuries sustained during World War II.

The Julia figure is transmogrified in *Toys in the Attic* along with Hellman's father and aunts. The entire play is a kind of dream displacement, as if the Hellmans had merged with the Newhouses and assumed their worst features. Julia's virtues (sharing of wealth, commitment to a cause) undergo a bizarre inversion as they are acquired by characters who turn them into vices. Instead of using money constructively as Julia did, Julian squanders it on pretentious gifts that alienate Carrie and make her his enemy. The victim of Julian's folly is Charlotte Warkins, also a Julia parody. Charlotte's face is slashed not because she is fighting fascism but because she has deceived her husband. And the cause of her disfigurement is the destructive naiveté of Julian's wife, an anti-Lilly in a play that is an "anti-Julia."

If Hellman has her way, we will never know Julia's identity. And would it really matter? Julia was a higher version of Lillian Hellman; she was everything to which the "aimless rebel," the "uncommitted" and "unfinished" woman aspired but never became. Julia was also Hellman's tribute to Dashiell Hammett, who lived by his principles as Julia lived by hers, expecting no recognition for doing what was right and deflating the egos of those who wanted it—he once told Howard Fast, who boasted that he was going to jail, that he would get more out of prison if he took off his crown of thorns. Most people find their models in books or movies. Hellman was fortunate; she found hers in life.

If "Julia" is Hellman's homage to the woman who was her moral teacher and the man who was her "closest, most beloved friend," *Julia* is Hollywood's homage to Lillian Hellman. Sargent and Zinnemann took a memoir that contained, in an unsophisticated, artless way, all the techniques of the new novel—spatial dislocations, temporal disjunctions, fusion of memories—and gave it a distinction it did not originally have. Yet they were faithful to Hellman's concept of the memoir as an attempt to confront the past by interleaving it with the present.

Julia was doubly significant; not only was it one of the most creative explorations of memory in the American film, but it was also one of the first American films to portray a genuine friendship between women. As far as women were concerned, a friend was rarely a second self in the typical Hollywood movie. As Molly Haskell has observed, "Male relationships are the ones that count."[10] Although women could embrace (while men could not) and dance together (while men could not), women still could not derive anything comparable to the knowledge-of-other that comes with friendship. Men occasionally could, in Westerns and war movies.

Knowledge-of-other begins in adolescence, but in the American film, adolescents were usually depicted as superficially as their relationships. When girls weren't studying together (*Junior Miss,* 1945) or talking pig Latin on the phone (*Janie,* 1944), they were mooning over boys (for example, *A Date with Judy,* 1948; *Two Weeks with Love,* 1950; *Bye Bye Birdie,* 1963; and the "Tammy" series). But they never quoted poetry or discussed social issues as Lilly and Julia did; and when they spoke of love, it was in the vernacular, not in lyrical improvisation.

Even middle-aged women in the movies could not enjoy the confluence of personalities that marks a lasting friendship. A woman had a buddy like Eve Arden, the type who constantly wisecracked to conceal her feelings. In *Mildred Pierce* (1945), when Mildred (Joan Crawford) stops at a restaurant for a cup of tea and then decides she wants a job, it is obvious that she and Ida (Eve Arden), the hostess, have much in common. Yet whatever they feel for each other is sublimated, if not submerged, in a routine relationship. Even when Mildred opens up her own restaurant chain and hires Ida, the situation does not change. Ida is part of the business and part of the household, but not part of Mildred's life.

When women were not business associates, they were rivals, either in love (Bette Davis and Mary Astor in *The Great Lie*, 1941) or professionally (Bette Davis and Miriam Hopkins in *Old Acquaintance*, 1943). In the latter, the two friends, a writer of quality fiction (Davis) and a pulp novelist (Hopkins), must have had something in common at one time, even if it were only professional rivalry. But rivalry is rarely stable; when it ceases to be professional, it becomes personal. *Old Acquaintance* is really a film of antifriendship, in which two women, who basically dislike each other, grow old together because they are loath to give up the joys of masochism, having become addicted to them at an early age.

In the movies of the 1930s and 1940s, men had a distinct advantage: they had Howard Hawks, who admitted that many of his films were love stories about men. Male bonding also had Hollywood's sanction. Men could seek each other out in time of crisis, especially during war, as happens in *The Dawn Patrol* (both the 1930 and 1938 versions), *Air Force* (1943), *Gung Ho* (1943), *Destination Tokyo* (1944), and *Halls of Montezuma* (1950). Isolation from women was another reason for men to enjoy the companionship of their own sex. During a cross-country cattle drive, a patriarch and his surrogate son, John Wayne and Montgomery Clift in Hawks's *Red River* (1948), find in each other what they cannot seem to find in women. And when Joanne Dru tells this Odysseus and Telemachus at the end of the film that they really love each other, she is not joking.

It would seem that what worked for men should also work for women, but this was not the case. Men who resolved their differences were mythic (Achilles and Agamemnon, Achilles and Priam); women were not, perhaps because there was no myth to cover their situation. In *Cry Havoc* (1943), two doomed nurses buried the hatchet before they walked out of their dugout to be taken prisoner by the Japanese. But the women never went beyond what they were—nurses in the Philippines during World War II.

Men in the classic Hollywood film could remain friends while at odds with each other, but women could not. A woman would be branded a bitch—or worse—if she did to her friend what an editor did to his star reporter in *The Front Page* (both the 1931 and 1974 versions)—namely, sabotage her friend's marriage the way Walter Burns sabotaged Hildy Johnson's. When Howard Hawks remade *The Front Page* as *His Girl Friday* (1940), he changed Hildy into a female (the name is androgynous); yet he kept the editor-reporter relationship amazingly platonic for a movie that featured Cary Grant as Walter and Rosalind Russell as Hildy. But could Hawks or anyone else at the time have reworked the plot to make both the editor and the reporter women? And could one woman have done to the other what Burns did to Hildy without antagonizing audiences who have grown up with the double standard?

Julia, then, was a breakthrough; it portrayed a friendship in various stages of development. But it was also a friendship between two intelligent women who wore their intelligence as gracefully as their womanhood. Lilly and Julia knew the warmth of proximity as they sat by a camp fire or lay on the floor, sipping wine and smoking; but they also knew the silences that come when words are inadequate to convey what is humanly ineffable.

Whether there will be more films like *Julia* is problematical. There have been other contemporary films about friendship between women—for example, *The Turning Point* (1977), *Voyage en Douce* (1980), and *Rich and Famous* (1981). However, the only valid comparison with *Julia* is not a movie but a play, Wendy Wasserstein's cinematically constructed *Uncommon Women and Others* (1978), which suggests that there is something special about relationships between educated women. It is not that they use more allusions or speak more articulately; rather, it is the way they interact with their feminine peers. They move to a gradual discovery of a common bond, not an epiphanic recognition culminating in a squeal of delight and a fluttery embrace. And when they experience rejection, it pains the mind as well as the emotions.

Even if *Julia* has no successors, it has at least given friendship between women a depth that has finally exceeded the dimensions of the screen.

Throughout her career as both playwright and screenwriter, Hellman has created women of strength, some less exemplary than others and only a few made of "sugar water," as Regina would say. It is unfortunate that she did not write more for both the stage and the screen. She certainly could have written more for the movies. In 1938, Hitchcock thought of her as a possibility for the screenplay of *Rebecca*.[11] She might also have done the screenplay of *A Streetcar Named Desire;* in her testimony to the House Committee on Un-American Activities, she stated that in 1948 or 1949, producer Irene Selznick asked her to write a treatment of Williams's play for submission to the Breen office. Hellman would have been ideal for *Sister Carrie*, but the blacklist intervened and also relegated the films she would have written for Harry Cohn to the abode of the might-have-beens. In *Scoundrel Time*, she recalled how, in 1953, she was in Rome working on the screenplay of a Nancy Mitford novel, something she "would never have touched in the old days," for Alexander Korda.[12] She completed the script, and although Korda liked it, he could not pay her; he was bankrupt. We also know from one of his memos that David O. Selznick submitted some of the dialogue that had been written for *Tender is the Night* (1962) to Hellman to ascertain if it had a Fitzgerald flavor.

"[Movies] can be a lot of fun when they go right," Hellman remarked in 1962. Hers generally did. At least she never had to lament, as Fitzgerald did when Joseph L. Mankiewicz revised his *Three Comrades* screenplay, "I'm a good writer—honest." Her scripts speak for themselves.

Notes

Preface

1. The most successful revivals have been of *The Little Foxes*—the 1967 Lincoln Center production with Anne Bancroft and the 1981 Broadway production with Elizabeth Taylor. The American Conservatory Theatre in San Francisco mounted productions of *The Little Foxes* in 1979 and *Another Part of the Forest* in 1980. The 1979–80 season witnessed three major revivals of *Watch on the Rhine:* the Long Wharf production in New Haven, the same production transferred to Broadway, and one at the Center Stage in Baltimore. *The Children's Hour* has always been a challenge to actresses, such as Patricia Neal and Kim Hunter, who costarred in the 1952 revival, and Joanne Woodward and Shirley Knight, who did the play in Stockbridge, Massachusetts in the summer of 1978. Although both *Days to Come* and *My Mother, My Father and Me* were flops, the WPA Theater in New York revived them in 1978 and 1980 respectively. *The Autumn Garden* was successfully revived by the Arena Stage in Washington in 1977, and *Toys in the Attic* by the McCarter Theater Company in Princeton in 1978. Only *The Searching Wind* has remained unrevived.

Chapter 1

1. Tom Dardis, *Some Time in the Sun: The Hollywood Years of Fitzgerald, Faulkner, Nathanael West, Aldous Huxley, and James Agee* (New York: Scribner's, 1976), p. 80.

2. Telephone interview with the author, 16 November 1979.

3. Aaron Latham, *Crazy Sundays: F. Scott Fitzgerald in Hollywood* (New York: Viking, 1971), p. 7.

4. Samuel Marx, *Mayer and Thalberg: The Make-Believe Saints* (New York: Random House, 1975), p. 215. The story about Follett's having received a Pulitzer Prize is inaccurate; whatever prize he received, it was not a Pulitzer.

5. Alvin H. Marill, *Samuel Goldwyn Presents* (New York: A. S. Barnes, 1976), p. 21.

6. Hellman to the author (13 February 1980).

7. Robert Stanley, *The Celluloid Empire: A History of the Motion Picture Industry* (New York: Hastings House, 1978), p. 277.

Chapter 2

1. Katherine Lederer, *Lillian Hellman* (Boston: Twayne, 1979), p. 23.

2. Axel Madsen, *William Wyler: The Authorized Biography* (New York: Crowell, 1973), p. 133. For a dissenting opinion, see Michael Anderegg, *William Wyler* (Boston: Twayne, 1979), p. 47.

3. Richard S. Randall, *Censorship of the Movies: The Social and Political Control of a Mass Medium* (Madison: University of Wisconsin Press, 1968), p. 206.

4. Madsen, p. 361.

Chapter 4

1. The credits for *The Little Foxes* read: "Screenplay: Lillian Hellman. Additional Scenes and Dialogue by Dorothy Parker, Arthur Kober, and Alan Campbell." Wyler recalls the script as being Hellman's alone, but because Dorothy Parker and her husband, Alan Campbell, needed money, she had their names added to the credits; see Madsen, pp. 207–8. According to Richard Moody, *Lillian Hellman, Playwright* (New York: Pegasus/Bobbs-Merrill, 1972), p. 113, Kober even wanted his name omitted.

2. According to Whitney Stine, *Mother Goddam: The Story of Bette Davis* (New York: Hawthorn Books, 1974), p. 149, Kober and the Campbells created the character of "David Hewlitt" *(sic)*. One suspects that was all they did.

3. Gordon to the author (17 March 1980).

Chapter 5

1. Margaret Case Harriman, *Take Them Up Tenderly: A Collection of Profiles* (New York: Knopf, 1945), p. 104.

2. On the connection between Breda and Kurt, see Larry Ceplair and Steven Englund, *The Inquisition in Hollywood: Politics in the Film Community, 1930–1960* (Garden City, N.Y.: Anchor Press/Doubleday, 1980), p. 106. It is also possible that the name of Bodo, the youngest of the Müller children, was inspired by Bodo Uhse, the German Communist writer who fought in the Spanish Civil War and later lived in exile in Mexico.

3. Manfred Triesch, *The Lillian Hellman Collection at the University of Texas* (Austin, Tex.: Humanities Research Center, 1966), p. 31.

4. Hugh Thomas, *The Spanish Civil War*, rev. ed. (New York: Harper & Row, 1977), p. 455.

5. Gerald Rabkin, *Drama and Commitment: Politics in the American Theatre of the Thirties* (Bloomington: Indiana University Press, 1964), p. 27.

6. Charles Higham, *Warner Brothers* (New York: Scribner's 1975), p. 148.

7. Arthur Marx, *Goldwyn: A Biography of the Man behind the Myth* (New York: Norton, 1976), p. 293, is incorrect in stating that after her falling out with Goldwyn, Hellman "even went so far as to sell her next hit play, *Watch on the Rhine*, to Warner Brothers." In December 1941, Hellman and Goldwyn were still on good terms.

8. Hellman had every intention of being involved in the film: "She believes better results can be obtained if she is in the studio for consultation" (telegram from Wilk to Wallis, 7 April 1942, Warner Achive, University of Southern California, Los Angeles). Initially, Wallis wondered if her contract with Goldwyn would pose a problem, but apparently Goldwyn had no objection.

9. This is known from a memo from Wallis to Hellman (21 May 1942) requesting dialogue for the scene (Warner Archive).

10. Whitney Stine, *Mother Goddam: The Story of Bette Davis* (New York: Hawthorn Books, 1974), p. 171.

11. In his autobiography *Starmaker* (New York: Macmillan, 1980), p. 108, Wallis acknowledged the script as Hammett's, calling it "very fine work."

12. The prologue seems to have been written by Wallis, who sent the text to the editor, Rudi Fehr, in the form of a memo (31 August 1942, Warner Archive) the day before the final cut was completed. The first sentence of the prologue was struck out: "For almost seven months armies on the Western Fronts had waited." Wallis may have thought that too much

chronology would be burdensome and that a reference to the "phony war" or *Sitzkrieg* of the fall and winter of 1939–40 would be inappropriate in 1942–43.

13. Breen to Warner (29 May 1942, Warner Archive).

14. Bernard Rosenberg and Harry Silverstein, *The Real Tinsel* (New York: Macmillan, 1979), p. 370.

Chapter 6

1. Eric Bentley ed., *Thirty Years of Treason: Excerpts from Hearings before the House Committee on Un-American Activities, 1938–1968* (New York: Viking, 1971), p. 112.

2. Hellman should not have set the action in the Ukraine, where Communism was generally unpopular. Photographs show the Ukrainians initially greeting the Germans as liberators; see James L. Stokesbury, *A Short History of World War II* (New York: Morrow, 1980), pp. 156–57; C. L. Sulzberger, *The American Heritage Picture History of World War II* (American Heritage Publishing Co., 1966), p. 259. However, the historical details that her researcher Lelia Alexander provided were accurate (the bleeding to death of children in Poland and Russia; the Soviet aviators who crash-dived, kamikaze style, into Nazi supply lines).

3. Although Copland has vivid memories of his scores for *The Red Pony* (1949) and *The Heiress* (1949), he has none of *The North Star:* "I wish I could send you some pertinent reflections on the writing of the musical score. . . . I confess however that the passage of time has rather dimmed my memories of specific events and associations with that particular film" (Copland to the author, 21 April 1981).

Chapter 8

1. Doris V. Falk, *Lillian Hellman* (New York: Ungar, 1978), p. 90.

2. Robin Wood, *Arthur Penn* (New York: Praeger, 1969), p. 138. Wood also claims that, apart from the credits sequence, "what is on the screen was all shot by Penn."

3. Jeff Brown, "The Making of a Movie," *Holiday*, February 1966, p. 94.

4. Foote to the author (24 November 1979).

5. Hellman to the author (13 February 1980).

Chapter 9

1. Gene D. Phillips, "Fred Zinnemann: An Interview," *Journal of Popular Film*, 7 (1978): 65.

Chapter 10

1. Michiko Kakutani, "Hellman-McCarthy Libel Suit Stirs Old Antagonisms," *New York Times*, 19 March 1980, Section C, p. 21.

2. In *Shadow Man: The Life of Dashiell Hammett* (New York: Harcourt Brace Jovanovich, 1981), p. 136, Richard Layman lays this charge to rest: "Hellman's work was entirely her own and the irresponsible charge sometimes made that Hammett was her collaborator is false. Rather, he influenced her by his strict literary standards." Another irresponsible charge, mentioned by Raymond Chandler in a 1945 letter, is that Hammett's "screenwriting

jobs" were done by "La Hellman"; see *Selected Letters of Raymond Chandler*, ed. Frank MacShane (New York: Columbia University Press, 1981), p. 53. The charge is absurd since Hammett has only one screenplay credit, *Watch on the Rhine*, although he had a reputation for polishing the screenplays of others.

3. "A New Kind of McCarthyism: Actor Kevin Interviews Sister Mary on Her Books, Loves, and Life," *People Weekly*, 12 November 1979, p. 99.

4. Ibid.

5. Diana Trilling, *We Must March My Darlings: A Critical Decade* (New York: Harcourt Brace Jovanovich, 1977), p. 46.

6. Philip Dunne, *Take Two: A Life in Movies and Politics* (New York: McGraw-Hill, 1980), p. 188.

7. Martha Gellhorn, "On Apocryphism," *Paris Review* 23, no. 79 (Spring 1981): 280–301.

8. Larry Ceplair and Steven Englund, *The Inquisition in Hollywood: Politics in the Film Community, 1930–1960* (Garden City, N.Y.: Anchor Press/Doubleday, 1980), p. 115.

9. Clive James, "It Is of a Windiness: Lillian Hellman," in *At the Pillars of Hercules* (London: Faber & Faber, 1979), p. 174.

10. Molly Haskell, *From Reverence to Rape: The Treatment of Women in the Movies* (Baltimore, Md.: Penguin Books, 1974), p. 23.

11. *Memo from David O. Selznick*, selected and edited by Rudy Behlmer (New York: Avon Books, 1973), p. 303.

12. Hellman never specified the title of Mitford's novel, but it was *The Blessing* (1951); see Michael Korda, *Charmed Lives: A Family Romance* (New York: Random House, 1979), p. 383. The script is in the Lillian Hellman Collection at the University of Texas, Austin.

Selected Bibliography

Primary Sources

Foote, Horton. *The Chase: A Play in Three Acts*. New York: Dramatists Play Service, 1952.

———. *The Chase*. New York: Rinehart and Co., 1956.

———. *Harrison, Texas: Eight Television Plays*. New York: Harcourt, Brace, 1956.

Hammett, Dashiell. *Watch on the Rhine* (Screenplay). In *Best Film Plays 1943–44*, edited by John Gassner and Dudley Nichols. 1945. Reprint. New York: Garland, 1977.

Kingsley, Sidney. *Dead End*. In *Sixteen Famous American Plays*, edited by Bennett Cerf and Van H. Cartmell. New York: Random House, 1941.

Trevelyan, H. B. (Guy Bolton). *The Dark Angel: A Play of Yesterday and Today*. London: Ernest Benn, 1928.

Works of Lillian Hellman
(in chronological order)

Plays

The Children's Hour. New York: Random House, 1934.

Days to Come. New York: Random House, 1936.

The Little Foxes. New York: Random House, 1939.

Watch on the Rhine. New York: Random House, 1941.

The Searching Wind. New York: Viking, 1944.

Another Part of the Forest. New York: Viking, 1947.

Montserrat. New York: Dramatists Play Service, 1950.

The Autumn Garden. Boston: Little, Brown, 1951.

The Lark. New York: Random House, 1956.

Candide. New York: Random House, 1957.

Toys in the Attic. New York: Random House, 1960.

My Mother, My Father and Me. New York: Random House, 1961.

The Collected Plays. Boston: Little, Brown, 1972.

Screenplay

The North Star: A Motion Picture about Some Russian People. New York: Viking, 1943.

Editions with Introductions

The Selected Letters of Anton Chekhov. New York: Farrar, Straus, and Cudahy, 1955.

The Big Knockover: Selected Stories and Short Novels by Dashiell Hammett. New York: Random House, 1966.

Memoirs

An Unfinished Woman. Boston: Little, Brown, 1969.

Pentimento: A Book of Portraits. Boston: Little, Brown, 1973.

Scoundrel Time. Boston: Little, Brown, 1976.

Three. Boston: Little, Brown, 1979. (The collected memoirs with new commentaries by Hellman and an introduction by Richard Poirier)

Story

Maybe. Boston: Little, Brown, 1980.

Secondary Sources

Anderegg, Michael. *William Wyler*. Boston: Twayne, 1979.

Adler, Jacob H. *Lillian Hellman*. Austin, Tex.: Steck-Vaughn, 1969.

Bentley, Eric, ed. *Thirty Years of Treason: Excerpts from Hearings before the House Committee on Un-American Activities, 1938–1968*. New York: Viking, 1971.

Bergman, Andrew. *We're in the Money: Depression America and Its Films*. New York: New York University Press, 1971.

Bills, Steven H. *Lillian Hellman: An Annotated Bibliography*. New York: Garland, 1979.

Brown, Jeff. "The Making of a Movie." *Holiday*, February 1966, p. 87.

Canham, Kingsley. "Lewis Milestone." In *The Hollywood Professionals*. Vol. 2. New York: A. S. Barnes, 1974.

Ceplair, Larry, and Englund, Steven. *The Inquisition in Hollywood: Politics and the Film Community, 1930–1960*. Garden City, N.Y.: Anchor Press/Doubleday, 1980.

Dardis, Tom. *Some Time in the Sun: The Hollywood Years of Fitzgerald, Faulkner, Nathanael West, Aldous Huxley, and James Agee*. New York: Scribner's, 1976.

Dick, Bernard F. "Lillian Hellman." In *American Writers*. Supplement 1, pt. 1. New York: Scribner's, 1979.

Drutman, Irving. "Questioning Miss Hellman on Movies." *New York Times*, 27 February 1966, Section 2, p. 5.

Dunne, Philip. *Take Two: A Life in Movies and Politics*. New York: McGraw-Hill, 1980.

Easton, Carol. *The Search for Sam Goldwyn: A Biography*. New York: William Morrow, 1976.

Estrin, Mark W. *Lillian Hellman: A Reference Guide*. Boston: G. K. Hall, 1980.

Falk, Doris V. *Lillian Hellman*. New York: Frederick Ungar, 1978.

Ferris, Susan. "The Making of *Julia*." *Horizon*, October 1977, pp. 86–94.

Gellhorn, Martha. "On Apocryphism." *Paris Review* 23, no. 79 (Spring 1981): 280–301.

Latham, Aaron. *Crazy Sundays: F. Scott Fitzgerald in Hollywood*. New York: Viking, 1971.

Layman, Richard. *Shadow Man: The Life of Dashiell Hammett*. New York: Harcourt Brace Jovanovich, 1981.

Lederer, Katherine. *Lillian Hellman*. Boston: Twayne, 1979.

Madsen, Axel. *William Wyler: The Authorized Biography*. New York: Crowell, 1973.

Mancia, Adrienne, ed. *Hal B. Wallis, Film Producer*. New York: Museum of Modern Art, 1970.

Marill, Alvin H. *Samuel Goldwyn Presents*. New York: A. S. Barnes, 1976.

Marx, Arthur. *Goldwyn: A Biography of the Man behind the Myth*. New York: Norton, 1976.

Marx, Samuel. *Mayer and Thalberg: The Make-Believe Saints*. New York: Random House, 1975.

Moody, Richard. *Lillian Hellman, Playwright*. New York: Pegasus/Bobbs-Merrill, 1972.

Navasky, Victor S. *Naming Names*. New York: Viking, 1980.

Phillips, Gene D. "Fred Zinnemann: An Interview." *Journal of Popular Film and Television* 7 (1978): 56–66.

Rosenberg, Bernard, and Silverstein, Harry. *The Real Tinsel*. New York: Macmillan, 1970.

Roughead, William. *Bad Companions*. New York: Duffield and Green, 1931.

Sherman, Eric, and Rubin, Martin. *The Director's Event: Interviews with Five American Film-Makers*. New York: Atheneum, 1970.

Stine, Whitney. *Mother Goddam: The Story of Bette Davis*. New York: Hawthorn Books, 1974.

Strauss, Theodore. "The Author's Case: Post-Premiere Cogitations of Lillian Hellman on *The North Star*." *New York Times*, 19 December 1943, section 2, p. 5.

Triesch, Manfred. *The Lillian Hellman Collection at the University of Texas*. Austin, Tex.: Humanities Research Center, 1966.

Trilling, Diana. *We Must March My Darlings: A Critical Decade*. New York: Harcourt Brace Jovanovich, 1977.

Wallis, Hal, and Higham, Charles. *Starmaker: The Autobiography of Hal Wallis*. New York: Macmillan, 1980.

Wood, Robin. *Arthur Penn*. New York: Praeger, 1969.

Filmography
(in chronological order)

The Dark Angel (United Artists, 1935)
Director: Sidney Franklin
Producer: Samuel Goldwyn
Screenplay: Lillian Hellman and Mordaunt Shairp, from the play by Guy Bolton
Photography: Gregg Toland
Musical director: Alfred Newman
Released: Fall 1935
Running time: 105 minutes
16mm rental: Audio Brandon
Cast: Fredric March (Alan Trent), Merle Oberon (Kitty Vane), Herbert Marshall (Gerald Shannon), Janet Beecher (Mrs. Shannon), John Halliday (Sir George Barton)

These Three (United Artists, 1936)
Director: William Wyler
Producer: Samuel Goldwyn
Screenplay: Lillian Hellman
Photography: Gregg Toland
Music: Alfred Newman
Released: Spring 1936
Running time: 90 minutes
16mm rental: Audio Brandon
Cast: Merle Oberon (Karen Wright), Miriam Hopkins (Martha Dobie), Joel McCrea (Dr. Joe Cardin), Alma Kruger (Mrs. Tilford), Bonita Granville (Mary Tilford)

Dead End (United Artists, 1937)
Director: William Wyler
Producer: Samuel Goldwyn
Screenplay: Lillian Hellman, from the play by Sidney Kingsley
Photography: Gregg Toland
Music: Alfred Newman
Released: Summer 1937
Running time: 93 minutes
16mm rental: Audio Brandon
Cast: Sylvia Sidney (Drina), Joel McCrea (Dave), Humphrey Bogart

(Baby Face Martin), Wendy Barrie (Kay), Claire Trevor (Francey), Marjorie Main (Mrs. Martin), Billy Halop (Tommy), Huntz Hall (Dippy), Bobby Jordan (Angel), Leo Gorcey (Spit), Gabriel Dell (T.B.)

The Little Foxes (RKO, 1941)
Director: William Wyler
Producer: Samuel Goldwyn
Screenplay: Lillian Hellman
Additional Scenes and Dialogue: Arthur Kober, Dorothy Parker, Alan Campbell
Photography: Gregg Toland
Music: Meredith Wilson
Released: August 1941
Running time: 116 minutes
16mm rental: Audio Brandon
Cast: Bette Davis (Regina Giddens), Herbert Marshall (Horace Giddens), Teresa Wright (Alexandra), Patricia Collinge (Birdie), Dan Duryea (Leo), Charles Dingle (Ben), Carl Benton Reid (Oscar), Richard Carlson (David Hewitt)

Watch on the Rhine (Warner Bros., 1943)
Director: Herman Shumlin
Producer: Hal B. Wallis
Screenplay: Dashiell Hammett
Additional Scenes and Dialogue: Lillian Hellman
Photography:Merritt Gerstad and Hal Mohr
Music: Max Steiner
Released: September 1943
Running time: 114 minutes
16mm rental: UA/16
Cast: Bette Davis (Sara Müller), Paul Lukas (Kurt Müller), Geraldine Fitzgerald (Marthe de Brancovis), George Coulouris (Teck), Lucile Watson (Fanny Farrelly), Donald Woods (David), Eric Roberts (Bodo), Donald Buka (Joshua)

The North Star (RKO, 1943)
Director: Lewis Milestone
Producer: Samuel Goldwyn
Associate Producer: William Cameron Menzies
Original story and screenplay: Lillian Hellman
Photography: James Wong Howe
Music: Aaron Copland
Lyrics: Ira Gershwin
Dance: David Lichine
Released: November 1943
Running time: 105 minutes
16mm rental: Audio Brandon

Cast: Anne Baxter (Marina), Dana Andrews (Kolya), Walter Huston (Dr. Kurin), Walter Brennan (Karp), Ann Harding (Sophia), Jane Withers (Clavdia), Farley Granger (Damian), Erich von Stroheim (Von Harden), Dean Jagger (Rodion), Eric Roberts (Grisha), Martin Kosleck (Dr. Richter), Ruth Nelson (Nadya)

The Searching Wind (Paramount, 1946)
Director: William Dieterle
Producer: Hal B. Wallis
Screenplay: Lillian Hellman
Photography: Lee Garmes
Music: Victor Young
Released: Summer 1946
Running time: 108 minutes
16mm rental: Swank
Cast: Robert Young (Alex Hazen), Sylvia Sidney (Cassie Bowman), Ann Richards (Emily), Dudley Digges (Moses), Douglas Dick (Sam)

Another Part of the Forest (Universal-International, 1948)
Director: Michael Gordon
Producer: Jerry Bresler
Screenplay: Vladimir Pozner
Photography: Hal Mohr
Music: Daniele Amfitheatrof
Released: Spring 1948
Running time: 107 minutes
16mm rental: Universal/16
Cast: Fredric March (Marcus Hubbard), Florence Eldridge (Lavinia), Dan Duryea (Oscar), Edmond O'Brien (Ben), Ann Blyth (Regina), John Dall (John Bagtry)

The Children's Hour (United Artists, 1962)
Director: William Wyler
Producer: William Wyler
Screenplay: John Michael Hayes
Adaptation: Lillian Hellman
Photography: Franz F. Planer
Music: Alex North
Released: March 1962
Running time: 107 minutes
16mm rental: UA/16
Cast: Audrey Hepburn (Karen Wright), Shirley MacLaine (Martha Dobie), James Garner (Dr. Joe Cardin), Miriam Hopkins (Mrs. Mortar), Fay Bainter (Mrs. Amelia Tilford), Karen Balkin (Mary), Veronica Cartwright (Rosalie)

Toys in the Attic (United Artists, 1963)
Director: George Roy Hill

Producer: Walter Mirisch
Screenplay: James Poe
Photography: Joseph Biroc
Music: George Dunning
Released: June 1963
Running time: 88 minutes
16mm rental: UA/16
Cast: Dean Martin (Julian Berniers), Geraldine Page (Carrie), Yvette Mimieux (Lily), Wendy Hiller (Anna), Gene Tierney (Albertine Prine)

The Chase (Columbia, 1966)
Director: Arthur Penn
Producer: Sam Spiegel
Screenplay: Lillian Hellman, based on a novel and play by Horton Foote
Photography: Joseph La Shelle and (uncredited) Robert Surtees
Music: John Barry
Main Title: Maurice Bender
Released: February 1966
Running time: 135 minutes
16mm rental: Audio Brandon
Cast: Marlon Brando (Calder), Jane Fonda (Anna), Robert Redford (Bubber), E. G. Marshall (Val Rogers), James Fox (Jake Rogers), Miriam Hopkins (Mrs. Reeves), Angie Dickinson (Ruby), Janice Rule (Emily Stewart), Robert Duvall (Edwin Stewart), Martha Hyer (Mary Fuller), Richard Bradford (Damon Fuller), Diana Hyland (Elizabeth Rogers), Henry Hull (Briggs)

Julia (Twentieth Century-Fox, 1977)
Director: Fred Zinnemann
Producer: Richard Roth
Screenplay: Alvin Sargent, based upon the story by Lillian Hellman
Photography: Douglas Slocombe
Music: George Delerue
Released: Fall 1977
Running time: 118 minutes
16mm rental: Films, Inc.
Cast: Jane Fonda (Lillian), Vanessa Redgrave (Julia), Jason Robards (Hammett), Maximilian Schell (Johann), Rosemary Murphy (Dottie), Hal Holbrook (Alan), Meryl Streep (Anne-Marie), Lisa Pelikan (Young Julia), Susan Jones (Young Lillian)

Index